FABIAN SOCIE

G000270665

The Fabian Society is Britain's leading left of centre think tank and political society, committed to creating the political ideas and policy debates which can shape the future of progressive politics.

With over 300 Fabian MPs, MEPs, Peers, MSPs and AMs, the Society plays an unparalleled role in linking the ability to influence policy debates at the highest level with vigorous grassroots debate among our growing membership of over 7000 people, 70 local branches meeting regularly throughout Britain and a vibrant Young Fabian section organising its own activities. Fabian publications, events and ideas therefore reach and influence a wider audience than those of any comparable think tank. The Society is unique among think tanks in being a thriving, democratically-constituted membership organisation, affiliated to the Labour Party but organisationally and editorially independent.

For over 120 years Fabians have been central to every important renewal and revision of left of centre thinking. The Fabian commitment to open and participatory debate is as important today as ever before as we explore the ideas, politics and policies which will define the next generation of progressive politics in Britain, Europe and around the world.

Fabian Society
11 Dartmouth Street
London SW1H 9BN
www.fabians.org.uk

First published 2009
ISBN 978 0 7163 4106 2

Editorial Director: Tom Hampson
Editorial Manager: Ed Wallis

To find out more about the Fabian Society, the Young
Fabians, the Fabian Women's Network and our local
societies, please visit our web site at **www.fabians.org.uk**.

From the Workhouse to Welfare

What Beatrice Webb's 1909 Minority Report can teach us today

Edited by Ed Wallis

FABIAN SOCIETY   Webb Memorial Trust

Fighting Poverty and Inequality in an Age of Affluence

Beatrice Webb's 1909 Minority Report to the Poor Law Commission first set out the vision, arguments and values of social justice that were to become the foundations of the modern welfare state. It challenged the dominant assumption that the poor were solely to blame for their own poverty, demonstrating that the causes of poverty are structural as well as individual, and argued that society has a collective responsibility to prevent poverty, not merely alleviate it.

Culminating in 2009, Fighting poverty and inequality in an age of affluence will commemorate the centenary of the Minority Report by making a major contemporary contribution to the strategy for fighting poverty and inequality in today's Britain.

At a time when arguments about the causes of poverty, the principles of social justice and the responsibilities of the state are again central and contested issues in our political discourse, the project will explore how the Minority Report's key insights should be renewed and applied today. In doing so, the project will set out some core principles of contemporary citizenship that should underpin a new welfare settlement for the 21st century, as well as a series of practical proposals that will make a real difference to tackling poverty and inequality.

For further information about the project's research programme, events and publications, please visit our web site at: www.fabians.org.uk/research/fightingpoverty

About the authors

Nick Bosanquet is Professor of Health Policy at Imperial College and Consultant Director of REFORM. He was Chairman of the Fabian Society from 1973-4 and councillor in the London Borough of Camden from 1974-82.

Jose Harris is Professor of Modern History at St Catherine's College Oxford and was a tutorial fellow in history at St Catherine's from 1978-97.

Roy Hattersley was MP for Birmingham Sparkbrook from 1964 to 1997 and Deputy Leader of the Labour Party from 1983 to 1992.

Dianne Hayter is Vice Chair of the Webb Memorial Trust and past General Secretary and Chair of the Fabian Society.

Tim Horton is Research Director at the Fabian Society.

Sunder Katwala is General Secretary of the Fabian Society.

Seema Malhotra is the Director of the Fabian Women's Network which she co-founded in 2005, and a campaigner on equality issues.

Peter Townsend is Professor of International Social Policy at the London School of Economics and Emeritus Professor of the University of Bristol. He is also Vice President of the Fabian Society.

Jon Trickett is Labour Member of Parliament for Hemsworth. He served as the Parliamentary Private Secretary to the Secretary of State for Trade and Industry in 1997 and from November 2008, has been the PPS to the Prime Minister.

Sarah Wise is the author of The Italian Boy: Murder and Grave Robbery in 1830s London, which was shortlisted for the 2005 Samuel Johnson Prize for Non-Fiction and won the Crime Writers' Association Gold Dagger for Non-Fiction. Her follow-up, The Blackest Streets, was published in June 2008.

Ed Wallis is Editorial Manager at the Fabian Society.

CONTENTS

INTRODUCTION 1
Sunder Katwala

1. A SHORT GUIDE TO THE MINORITY REPORT 9
Tim Horton

2. ONLY EQUALITY CAN STOP HISTORY 21
REPEATING
Roy Hattersley

3. POVERTY AND THE WORKHOUSE 27
Sarah Wise

4. AN UNJUST LAW 37
Jon Trickett

5. FROM PHILANTHROPY TO POLITICS 47
Dianne Hayter

6. THE WEBBS AND BEVERIDGE 55
Jose Harris

7. BEYOND BEATRICE 65
Seema Malhotra

8. IN PRAISE OF THE MAJORITY REPORT 71
Nick Bosanquet

9. THE 2009 MINORITY REPORT ON THE 77
WORLD BANK
Peter Townsend

Beatrice Webb in the spring of 1900

The Passfield Collection, LSE

INTRODUCTION

Sunder Katwala

I f we remember the dreaded workhouse today, it is often as we watch the creations of Dickens or Hardy struggle to escape the cruel twists of fortune in the latest BBC costume drama. The past is another country. Those authors intended to move and anger their contemporaries, but the workhouse's manifest cruelty makes it an inexplicable social institution to us. We slip easily into thinking that it was swept away by some inevitable Whiggish evolution of our modern world, and that those who opposed change were gargoyles like Mr Bumble and Mr Gradgrind: caricatures served up for our amusement before finally getting their just deserts.

That is not what happened. Social change does not happen by chance. Abolishing the workhouse required heretical new ideas, fierce political arguments and dogged campaigns. It was resisted seriously and successfully, and by liberal reformers as well as those with most at stake in the entrenched order of things.

That is why the story of Beatrice Webb's 1909 Minority Report on the Poor Law begins as a study in political failure. She failed to convince the Majority of the Royal Commission

1

to back the argument of the Minority quarter; she failed to get the Liberal Government to adopt her vision, or even to pursue those modest ameliorative reforms she had persuaded the Majority to adopt; and failed again in the Fabian-led civic Campaign for the Abolition of the Poor Law's attempt to challenge the political elite from below.

But this was perhaps the most important failure in welfare history and the history of British political ideas. The Minority Report mattered, and should matter still, because it began a new public argument about the causes of poverty, about responsibility for preventing it and, by extension, about the nature of citizenship. Those arguments continue today.

The Minority Report was too utopian a vision for 1909. It was no idle tilting at windmills but a particular, very practical utopianism. Any modern reader attempting the Minority Report finds a painstakingly researched deconstruction of the failures of the New Poor Law and a detailed account of the administrative challenges in the Webb's alternative scheme. In this it reflects Denis Healey's affectionately mocking tribute, in *New Fabian Essays* of 1951, to how the early Fabians "found socialism wandering aimlessly in Cloud Cuckoo Land and set it working on the gas and water problems of the nearest town or village. The modern Welfare State is their monument."

Yet this also misses the point. What endures from the Minority Report is not the technocratic under-wiring of how a modern welfare system of universal healthcare, minimum wages, labour exchanges and unemployment assistance would operate but, as Tim Horton sets out in chapter 1, the somewhat buried philosophical account about why such provision must become a core condition of social citizenship. In this, Beatrice Webb offers the first articulation of the core principles, and many of the central recommendations too, which underpinned the Beveridge Report of

1942, the founding document of the 'People's Peace' which the post-war welfare consensus sought to enshrine.

There are legitimate criticisms to be made of the Beveridge Report; more still of its implementation; and above all of the failure to deepen the settlement or maintain the social consensus which underpinned it a generation later. Perhaps Beveridge and Attlee did more to address the problems of the 1930s than the 1960s, though that was no small achievement in itself: the post-war welfare settlement remains, by some distance, the greatest peacetime achievement of any British government. Those who want to counter that it was the great mistake of post-war British history, primarily responsible for relative economic decline (Correlli Barnett's argument which retains a hold on the post-Thatcherite right) never explain how democratic consent could have been secured for a return to business as usual after 1945.

The road from 1909 to 1942 involves personal as well as intellectual connections. Beveridge worked as a researcher on the Minority Report, writing in his memoirs that "the Beveridge Report stemmed from what all of us had imbibed from the Webbs". The part-time organiser of the anti-Poor Law campaign went on to be Labour's greatest Prime Minister, Clement Attlee, who four decades on, as the ashes of the Webbs were ceremoniously interred in Westminster Abbey, said that "millions are living fuller and freer lives today because of the work of Sidney and Beatrice Webb".

Yet how unfashionable the Webbs have become. If their influence is noted, it is usually to regret their dominance in shaping the politics of the 20th century British left and the welfare state. Beatrice Webb's achievement in 1909 must surpass the impact of any woman on British democratic politics prior to female suffrage, as Diane Hayter sets out in chapter 5. Yet, announced by convention as 'Mrs Sidney Webb' on the Minority Report frontispiece, our age of feminism and post-feminism has subsumed her into this double-headed, dual-brained phenomenon of 'the Webbs', psychologically distanced from us perhaps less by their ideas as by their all-but-overwhelming sense of public duty. How few remember that, in Bernard Crick's view, "Beatrice Webb must be numbered, however unexpectedly to some, among the great English diarists" with a rather greater capacity for gossip and intrigue than Roy Hattersley acknowledges in chapter 2. Sidney Webb's authorship of the 1918 clause four of Labour's constitution is taken to exemplify a commitment to socialism red in tooth and claw when, in its own time, this was the moderates' charter by which gradualist democratic socialism would rebut the challenge of the Bolshevik revolution.

So the Webbs have become a convenient shorthand to caricature the Fabian tradition as grey-on-grey statism, and not only for the right to target the egalitarian left. Making villains of 'the Webbs' has often suited many on their own side too, as part of the continual and vital debate within the plural Fabian left about the pursuit of moral as well as mechanical reform.

The shadow of Stalin looms large. The Webbs made a grave mistake, and no excuses should be made for it. They were among too many on right and left who made major political misjudgements about the dictators of the 1930s. When still more was known of the Gulag a few years later, Orwell's difficulty in having Animal Farm published reflected the closing of British establishment ranks against any criticism of Stalin after 1941. The relevance of the Webbs' later naivety – in their seventies – in failing to see beneath the official Soviet line, to a judgement of the value of their pioneering work of thirty years before can certainly be challenged.

But disentangling this matters, because the point of the charge is to prosecute the case that their later defection to Communism was no breach with their earlier Fabianism and democratic socialism, but a natural extension of it.

But this can not hold. The Webbs' advocacy of 1909 does not lead inexorably to Stalin. The triumph – though perhaps personal tragedy – of their Fabian gradualism was that their strategy of political arguments, education and institutional permeation did its work despite the defection of its founders. Beveridge's great report, Attlee's cabinet of 1945 and the arguments being extended by Richard Titmuss and Peter Townsend at the LSE brought about a quiet social revolution, even if the Webbs could not by then recognise the scale of their achievement.

To accept this at the level of ideas would leave only the choice offered by Hayek in *The Road to Serfdom*: that the only alternative to libertarianism will always lead to totalitarianism. That was rejected in 1945, and disproved in post-war Europe, yet the hard point arising from the 1909 Minority Report is still usually evaded in contemporary debate about the role of the state. The central question is not what the state should provide, but what the state must guarantee as the 'basic minimum' and a condition of citizenship. The contested issue is rarely whether there should be any basic minimum at all. After all, the Poor Law itself reflects the commitment – going back to 1600 in England – to some collective responsibility, albeit to prevent starvation and ensure basic subsistence, not the means of social participation. What the Minority Report insists on is that citizenship is only meaningful if the poor are treated as equal citizens, not grateful supplicants. This idea of equality of respect underpins their insistence on universal, not segregated, services. Their critique of the workhouse exemplifies Titmuss' argument fifty years later that services for the poor will always remain poor services; and that the NHS could survive, as much of the post-war settlement was ditched, offers important truths about how universalism best entrenches progressive change.

An analysis of poverty, however well-meaning, rooted primarily in individual behavioural causes within the 'underclass' fails to understand this. No doubt the moralistic counter-argument will never go away: that accepting our collective responsibility ignores the moral failings of the individual, and that self-help must be central. The Webbs' evidence proved in 1909 that this had been tried, had failed, and that it kept people in the poverty trap of the workhouse. Self-evidently, the outcome was hardly sturdy independence but the broken self-respect and dependency culture of those stigmatised by the need to rely on charitable provision which proved deeply inadequate in providing even basic relief, to say nothing of prevention or cure.

A critique of statism which understands this foundational point about collective responsibility for an adequate minimum is very different from one which does not. Certainly Crosland's generation, seeking a new Fabianism that could lead a social democratic revisionism of the 1950s, believed a public reaction against the Webb tradition was needed. Yet whilst Crosland's famous liberal flourish in *The Future of Socialism* about "total abstinence and a good filing system" not being the signposts to the socialist Utopia is endlessly quoted, the argument that he stood on their shoulders to make it is always ignored. Crosland pays warm personal tribute to the Webbs and believes that the left now takes their public virtues for granted: "we have all, so to speak, been trained at the LSE, are familiar with blue books and white papers, and know our way around Whitehall. We realise ... that hard work and research are virtues ... That Fabian pamphlets must be diligently studied. We know these things too well. Posthumously, the Webbs have won their battle and converted a generation to their standards. Now the time has come for a reaction".

At the start of 2009, that a different rebalancing is needed is universally acknowledged; what that should entail is much less clear. If we have been reminded that the market has limits too and that the state has a necessary place, any political project, whether of left, right or centre, must surely dig deeper and find more to say than that. The Webbs forged a left which would understand the necessity of the state to achieve progressive ends. That lesson should not be forgotten, but it is important to know more than one thing. 1909 should also be reclaimed as part of a progressive tradition of radical ideas allied to movement politics. The early Fabian vision of educating, agitating and organising for change may once have seemed less urgent after the achievement of the Beveridge settlement. That it should be recovered today can surely not be in doubt.

"Winston and his wife dined here the other night to meet a party of young Fabians. He is taking on the look of the mature statesman – bon vivant and orator, somewhat in love with his own phrases. He did not altogether like the news of our successful agitation. 'You should leave the work of converting the country to us, Mrs Webb, you ought to convert the Cabinet.' 'That would be all right if we wanted merely a change in the law; but we want' I added, 'to really change the mind of the people with regard to the facts of destitution, to make them feel the infamy of it and the possibility of avoiding it. That won't be done by converting the Cabinet, even if we could convert the Cabinet – which I doubt. We will leave that task to a converted country!'"

– *Diary of Beatrice Webb, October 3rd, 1909*

1. A SHORT GUIDE TO THE MINORITY REPORT

Tim Horton

Tim Horton sketches the history of Beatrice Webb's 1909 Minority Report and draws out the key reasons why it still matters in 2009.

"The work should be both irksome and unskilled... You have got to find work which anybody can do, and which nearly everybody dislikes doing... You have got to give him something like corn-grinding or flint-crushing, cross-cut sawing, or some work of that sort, which is laborious and wholly unskilled."

James Stewart Davy, chief inspector of the Poor Law Division of the Local Government Board, succinctly and ruthlessly set out the principles of the workhouse in giving evidence to the 1905-9 Royal Commission.

The New Poor Law of 1834 was a regressive social reform, arising from the earlier Royal Commission of 1832-34: it was a reform driven by anxiety that the existence of poor relief would tempt many that were otherwise self-sufficient to claim.

The default assumption was that the cause of destitution was the moral fault of the individual – a 'failing of character'. Poverty was generally seen as a voluntary condition, with the pauper not so much the victim as the perpetrator of his own distress. Deterrence and punishment were therefore to be central features of Poor Law relief.

Individuals were to be strictly categorised into the labouring classes on the one hand, and the pauper class on the other (the concept of the 'labouring poor' was dismissed). The requirement that the able-bodied pauper and his family must be given relief within the workhouse meant that the pauper was segregated from the independent poor, stigmatised and deprived of civil rights on entering the workhouse.

'Indoor relief' in the workhouse was consciously made as unpleasant as possible, with hard labour (other common tasks included bone crushing and oakum picking), harsh and distressing regulations, the separation of married couples, the provision of bad food and poor diets, as well as strict discipline and a lack of social amenities.

Relief was designed to prevent starvation, not to prevent poverty. Its central principle of 'less eligibility' demanded that the condition of the able-bodied pauper must be kept inferior to that of the poorest independent labourer. This was seen as the 'just deserts' of those entering the workhouse, and was designed to force the pauper from the workhouse in search of whatever employment he could find on the open market. The unpleasant conditions were also taken as a self-imposed test of need: that the claimant was willing to submit to these privations rendered further investigation unnecessary.

Restricting eligibility for relief and the meagre provision arising from the principle of 'less eligibility' served another goal of reform in 1834: that of keeping the local taxation rates down. Rising expenditure on poor relief had been causing alarm for decades. A central emphasis of the system was getting people off the welfare rolls, regardless of their condition or resulting fate.

The Royal Commission

That the workhouse should be both feared and hated was the point of Poor Law relief. However, unrest over high unemployment in London in 1903-04 led Balfour's Conservative Government to establish the Royal Commission on the Poor Laws and the Relief of Distress, 1905-1909, to consider "whether any, and if so, what, modification of the Poor Laws or changes in their administration or fresh legislation for dealing with distress are advisable".

The 20 member Commission quickly polarised into what became its 'Majority' and 'Minority' factions. The Majority included the representatives of the Poor Law Division of the Local Government Board and the six members of the Charity Organisation Society, including Helen Bosanquet, who emphasised self-dependence and wanted to retain a leading role for charity in the relief of distress.

After Charles Booth had to withdraw on grounds of ill health, the Minority were comprised of a Fabian-Labour grouping of Beatrice Webb, George Lansbury and Francis Chandler and the Reverend Russell Wakefield.

What did the Minority Report argue?

Although the bulk of the text of the Minority Report is devoted to evidence about the shortcomings of the existing system and the administrative issues of the proposed reforms, the Webbs' critique of the New Poor Law went to the heart of the philosophical assumptions underpinning the system.

Poverty has structural causes

The Webbs' critique was founded in the observation that the causes of poverty and worklessness were 'structural' as well as individual. On many occasions these lay in the organisation of the economy and society, such as fluctuations in demand for labour, or in factors beyond an individual's control, such as ageing, illness, or a lack of nurture and education in infancy.

This was not just a challenge to the justice or relevance of a punitive system. It also helped to explain why the Poor Law had been so unsuccessful, with huge increases in inmates, claimants and expenditure through the 19th century. However tough it was on poverty, the Poor Law did nothing to address its causes.

The need for poverty prevention, rather than simply relief
A related criticism was that the whole system was focussed on 'relieving' distress once it had happened. A punitive system delayed assistance. But far from trying to stop people coming forward, the Webbs said society should be actively "searching them out" and dealing with them – just like a public health authority should do in the case of infectious disease.

The Webbs called for a systematic 'Framework of Prevention', with greater provision and action across areas such as health, education, old age, and the labour market. Tackling these causes meant shifting away from one institution – the workhouse – to deal with those who fell into poverty, and advocating differentiated services to deal with the particular causes of destitution and the particular needs of the individual.

The need for a curative rather than a deterrent system
The Webbs showed how, even on the Poor Law's own analysis of poverty – as representing a failure of individual character – it failed to tackle the problem. They noted that those administering the system reported that the

workhouse broke down the character of the individual, with the loss of self-respect and with it "the desire to rise again to true citizenship and individual responsibility."

Supporters of the Poor Law claimed to want to avoid 'dependency', yet the Webbs noted that making people 'less eligible' meant keeping people in poverty. This principle of 'less eligibility' also militated against specific interventions to promote independence, which the more benevolent Poor Law Guardians often wanted to do. For example, the New Poor Law refused to allow Boards of Guardians to continue an earlier practice of paying for tools and outfits for men and women trying to set up in trade, so trapping in the workhouse many who might have tried to make their own way in the world.

The responsibility of the state

Relocating the causes of poverty from individual moral fault to include structural and social conditions led the Webbs to advocate coordinated action by public authorities to fulfil the doctrine of prevention rather than relief.

They argued that the state had a duty to preserve certain standards below which no citizen should be allowed to fall. They used the slogan 'The National Minimum' to describe the political and social vision they were putting forward, which included a national minimum wage for those in work and adequate maintenance benefits for those out of work.

The Minority Report envisaged a large role for voluntary agencies working in partnership with government, but differed from the Majority Report in refusing to see these as an alternative to the state. In the Webbs' view, charities were seldom able to prevent destitution or distress by tackling their structural causes.

The need for universal – not segregated – services

The Webbs strongly rejected the division of service provision between the poor and the non-poor, which was both ineffective and designed to stigmatise.

Their prevention framework could not work without rejecting the idea of separate Poor Law services for paupers. Instead, they advocated the idea of universal services – organised around the functions of health, education and so on – and provided to all regardless of their status and without stigma. This was to be achieved by merging the Poor Law services with the existing services provided by local government committees.

That the 'pauper' and 'non-pauper' alike wanted the same types of services had already been demonstrated through the growing use of Poor Law medical services by wider sections of the population (something that made a mockery of the framework of deterrence). The Minority Report noted that: "In the more industrial quarters, the skilled artisans and the smaller shop-keepers are coming to regard the Poor Law infirmary... much as they do the public park or library – as a municipal institution, paid for by their rates, and maintained for their convenience and welfare."

The recommendations of the Minority Report

The purpose of the report, Beatrice Webb later claimed, was "to secure a national minimum of civilised life... open to all alike, of both sexes and all classes, by which we meant sufficient nourishment and training when young, a living wage when able-bodied, treatment when sick, and modest but secure livelihood when disabled or aged."

So the Minority Report saw the first advocacy of a scheme similar to the universal health service Britain enjoys today: "A Health Service having for its first great aim the prevention of disease, embracing the present Public Health, Medical Charities and Poor Law Hospital Services...would, I consider, particularly if managed as a state service, be a forward step of immense benefit to the public health and poor of the country."

Local authorities, through their health, education and asylum services, should provide the assistance needed by children, the sick, the aged and the mentally ill. The elderly should receive state pensions. These services were to be funded by a mixture of taxation and user charges, with need-based exemptions.

On unemployment, the Report called for "the whole problem of able-bodied destitution to be systematically dealt with by the National Government"; furthermore, "the duty of so organising the national labour market so as to prevent or minimise unemployment should be placed upon a minister responsible to Parliament, who might be designated the Minister for Labour."

The problem of low wages would be eliminated by a minimum wage. And the Report also argued for decent family support: "All mothers having the charge of young children, and in receipt, by themselves or their husbands, of any form of public assistance, should receive enough for the full maintenance of the family."

Finally, the Webbs were strong believers in conditionality. These services were not supposed to be one-way: they wanted people to feel a reciprocal obligation if they accepted a service. So a great deal of emphasis was placed on the recipient's obligation to co-operate with treatment, whether for sickness or unemployment, as a means of developing the social, economic and moral qualities of effective citizenship.

The Webbs did not hesitate to recommend enforcement, going so far as to advocate detention colonies, after a judicial process, for able-bodied people who refused either work or training. Their argument was that this would apply to the tiniest minority of cases, while the Poor Law failed to trust – and so stigmatised – those in genuine need. This element of compulsion as part of a social contract was another reason they advocated state, rather than charitable, provision. As Beatrice Webb later wrote to her sister, "we must have, behind all this good-will and expenditure, the element of compulsion and disciplinary supervision of the persons who are aided, and that could only be exercised by a public authority".

Where did the Minority and Majority Reports differ?

Beatrice Webb moved the Majority further from the principles of 1834 than it would have gone of its own accord. But central differences remained.

The retention of the Poor Law

The Majority Report would maintain the Destitution Authority, though it favoured reframing the 'Poor Law' as 'Public Assistance'. For the Webbs, this was simply rebranding. They insisted on the Poor Law being replaced by the newer specialised authorities already at work – for children by the local Education Committee, for the mentally ill by the Asylum Committee, and so on – dividing people not according to the presence or absence of destitution, but according to the services to be provided.

The role of charity and the state

The Majority Report wanted to give charitable bodies a primary role in social administration, with state action limited to exceptional cases. The Webbs believed that full responsibility for the policy and its execution should rest on the public authority, which should make use of voluntary agencies as it thought fit. The Majority's interest in charity was also focused on the desire to keep the rates – and public expenditure – down.

Deterrence and the causes of poverty

Beatrice Webb persuaded the Majority to move some way towards the concept of 'treating' pauperism and providing help. The Majority Report did countenance some preventative services: like the Minority Report, it proposed labour exchanges and unemployment insurance.

But the Charity Organisation Society, central among the Majority, continued to argue that the theory that destitution represented a 'failing of character' and that this principle must remain central to the operation of welfare. As Professor Bernard Bosanquet (husband of Majority Commission member Helen Bosanquet) put it: "the Majority proceed upon the principle that where there is a failure of social self-maintenance…there is a defect in the citizen character…which separates the treatment required by the destitute or necessitous from anything that can be offered to citizens who are maintaining themselves in a normal course of life."

The Minority Report: failure and vindication

Neither the Majority nor the Minority Report were directly influential on the Liberal Government to which they were presented, and the split Commission made it easier for the Government to resist pressure for reform.

Within a year, though, 25,000 copies of the Minority Report had been sold and the Treasury had to re-issue another edition. The Webbs' campaign organisation – The National Committee for the Break-up of the Poor Law –

won over almost all of the small Labour Parliamentary Party, which supported a private members' bill to make the case, but very few Liberals (with Winston Churchill a striking exception).

The Liberal Government resisted legislative reform of the Poor Law. Lloyd George was developing plans for unemployment and health insurance, and far from abolishing the Poor Law, decided to leave it unreformed, seeking instead to tackle poverty in a more piecemeal fashion.

A year after publication, it was evident the Webbs' campaign to have the Minority Report implemented was not going to succeed. The Majority Report was no longer the chief obstacle to reform: the Webbs' impact on it had made even this too radical for supporters of the status quo. And so the campaign reformed as the National Committee for the Prevention of Destitution, and it enlisted the more radical supporters of the Majority Report to fight the status quo, now focusing not on the abolition of the Poor Law Guardians but on the expansion of those public services which they recognised would ultimately undermine the Poor Law.

Politically, the Minority Report and the failure of the subsequent campaign resulted in an important realignment: it heralded the demise of Fabian attempts to influence the Liberal Party. Instead, they – and many like-minded individuals on the left – now focussed their attention on encouraging the growth of the Labour Party. And, in 1913, *The Crusade*, the Poor Law campaign's newsletter, became the *New Statesman*.

But much more of the Minority Report's argument was reflected in the post-1945 welfare settlement.

In fact, a central one of the Minority Report's recommendations was implemented during the First World

War, when a national Ministry of Labour was created in 1916, albeit mainly for administrative reasons. But the Webbs had to wait twenty years to see the Boards of Guardians and the workhouse abolished (Local Government Act 1929). And it wasn't until 1948 that the Poor Law was finally abolished through the National Assistance Act. The Act's first sentence was "The existing Poor Law shall cease to have effect".

A young William Beveridge had been employed by the Webbs as an adviser and researcher for the 1909 Commission, and had presented evidence to the Commission to push the idea of labour exchanges. Beveridge wrote to the Webbs on publication: "thanks for sending me the Utopian plan. I'm very glad to see it and still more glad to think that it will in due course be boomed. I'm much too much in agreement with it to have any criticisms to make."

His landmark report of 1942, which ushered in the post-war welfare state, incorporated and restated many Webb ideas – particularly the concept of a national minimum, guaranteed by the state, below which no citizen should fall. As TH Marshall, the renowned sociologist and historian of citizenship argued, the Webbs had provided the first comprehensive blueprint for a welfare state 'in embryo'. Their Minority Report could be seen as a "brilliant anticipation" of the eventual results of "a movement which had just begun and of which they sensed the nature".

Further reading

The following sources provide useful further reading about the 1909 Minority Report and were drawn on for the article above:

Englander, D. (1998) *Poverty and Poor Law Reform in 19th Century Britain, 1834-1914* (Longman: London)

Henriques, U. (1968) 'How cruel was the Victorian Poor Law?'. *Historical Journal*, vol.11

McBriar, A. (1962) *Fabian Socialism and English Politics, 1884-1918. (*London: Cambridge University Press)

Woodroofe, K. (1977) 'The Royal Commission on the Poor Laws, 1905-9. *International Review of Social History*, vol.22

2. ONLY EQUALITY CAN STOP HISTORY REPEATING

Roy Hattersley

What should progressives learn from their own history? Roy Hattersley says the left needs to make the moral case for greater equality in order to win the battles that remain from a century ago.

In the Labour Party, equality has always been a minority pursuit. The philosophers of social democracy – Tawney, Cole, Crosland and TH Green – were all egalitarians of one sort or another. And all of them wanted something more radical than the equality of opportunity - not the uniformity of equality of outcome but a change in the nature of society which reduced discrepancies in power and wealth. But most of the party itself – both membership and leadership – either ignored or rejected what should have been the keystone around which policy was built.

Part of the problem was the apparent (though not real) complexity of the equality argument. Demanding the nationalisation of the 'thousand major monopolies' was easy – even when, as in 1983, a thousand monopolies, of any sort, did not exist. Advocating equality required an excursion into ideology and Labour, as Dick Crossman wrote in *New Fabian Essays*, always regarded that as "dangerous Teutonic verbiage". Socialism, real 'old Labour' said, is about public ownership and added that people with doubts had only to read Clause Four of the 1918 party constitution which was printed on their membership cards.

For most of the Labour Party's life, equality was regarded as the 'revisionists' excuse' for flinching away from real socialism. The Tribune review of Tony Crosland's *Future of Socialism* was published under a headline that said it all: "And He Dares To Call This Socialism". Then, as a result of the Blairite Revolution (both cultural and continuous) the belief in greater equality was denounced as wild extremism. Meritocracy became the authorised version of Labour faith. Apparently its adherents did not know that the term was invented to describe a system with a callous disregard for the underprivileged and did not care that it amounted to patterns of shifting inequality. The new mantra which replaced Clause Four in the constitution is barely literate and generally meaningless. It commits the Labour Party to a series of platitudes with which no one could disagree.

Sidney Webb – the author of the 1918 constitution and of the commitment to "the ownership of the means of production, distribution and exchange" – should have known better. Not only ought he to have understood that socialism is about something more ennobling than economic organisation, he was in day-to-day touch with the attempt – also made in 1918 – to change national attitudes towards poverty as well as to alleviate its most vicious manifestation. Beatrice, his wife, was a member of a committee, set up and chaired by Lloyd George himself, to advise on a post-war social programme. By the autumn of 1917 it had evolved into a Ministry of Reconstruction working party which proposed a new policy on unemployment which Mrs Webb said "included all the conclusions of the (1909) Minority Report of the Poor Law Commission." Did the intellectually aggressive Beatrice never tell him that the ownership of industry was only important in so much as it affected the organisation of society? What else did they talk about in bed? Gossip, we are led to believe, was not their style.

The philosophical importance of the Minority Report, which in some ways transcended its practical proposals, was its assertion that poverty is not a crime and paupers were not guilty of an offence. That view admittedly owes something to what Tony Blair – criticising my assertion that there is a close correlation between deprivation and poor school perform-ance – once dismissed as "Marxist determinism". But we are all, to a greater or lesser degree, the victims or beneficiaries of our environment. The acceptance of that obvious truth was at the root of the Minority Report's rejection of the prin-ciple on which the Poor Law was based. The 1834 Poor Law Amendment Act had been explicit. To qualify for 'relief', a pauper must suffer "first the personal loss of reputation (which is understood by the stigma of pauperism itself), sec-ond the loss of personal freedom (which is secured by deten-tion in the workhouse) and third the loss of political freedom (which is secured by disenfranchisement)."

Since paupers had to be punished for their poverty, it is only reasonable to assume that the stern but just Victorians of 1834 believed the poor were guilty of an offence. They had failed to maintain themselves. In particular the unem-ployed were responsible for their unemployment. It is only fair to add that JS Davy – the head of the Poor Law Division of the Local Government Board and main oppo-nent of reform – conceded that there might be occasions when a man was out of work for reasons beyond his con-trol. But the need to deter the work-shy – who were sup-posed to make up the majority of the unemployed – required that he too must accept the due punishment. His dismissal of Beatrice Webb's alternative was part meta-physical and part heartless. "A man must stand by his acci-dents. He must suffer for the general good of the body politic" in order to "stem the tide of philanthropic impulse which was sweeping away the old embankment of deterrent tests for the receipt of relief".

That idea – considered in the context of the 1909 Royal Commission – sounds and is absurd. But while the language of the Poor Law is arcane, the idea is far from unfashionable a century later. I guarantee that millions of American Republicans still hold the view which Ronald Reagan put to me when, in 1976, he was on a 'swing round Europe' during his first, and unsuccessful, attempt to secure the presidential nomination. Nobody, he said, had to be unemployed. The Founding Fathers of the Great Republic had not asked for handouts. They had gone out into the wilderness, felled trees, planted corn and shot turkeys. Unemployment was a voluntary (lack of) activity which would be certainly reduced and possibly ended by making life less comfortable for the unemployed.

For the twenty-five years of the post-war consensus, almost everyone took it for granted that a vast majority of the unemployed wanted to work but were left on the dole by the economic failures of the system. The spirit of the Jarrow Crusade lived on in 'Marches for Jobs' every time a pit was closed or a factory announced redundancies. We all believed implicitly in the failure of demand for labour, rather than a failure of the will to work. And were right to do so. Perhaps now some of the stories about families who choose welfare are true. And among them there are, no doubt, layabouts who would rather sign on than clock in. But when I think of the young Afro-Caribbean boys who used to hang about street corners in what was once my constituency – deeply reluctant to work or train – I have no doubt that they too are more sinned against than sinning. Society has just failed them in a different way.

Once we accept that (more often than not) poverty is not to be blamed on the poor, there are only two possible rational responses to their plight. One is the now mercifully unacceptable argument that a percentage of families living below the poverty line is necessary for the flexibility of the economy. The other is that society, having caused their problem, has a duty to solve it. That requires resources, in one form or another, being re-routed in their direction – a process which, before the term became unfashionable, was called redistribution. And redistribution is the first battle in the war for greater equality.

There are other ways of helping the disadvantaged and the dispossessed. I have never objected to the coercive aspects of the welfare to work programme when it is applied to unemployed able-bodied young men as distinct from lone mothers. I welcome it as a long overdue rejection of John Stuart Mill's socially destructive nonsense about "all errors which (a man) is likely to commit against advice and warning are far outweighed by the evil of allowing others to constrain him for what they deem to be his own good." That assertion is at the heart of the mad individualism which has done so much harm to society over the last quarter of a century. But schemes to get the workless (and even the work-shy) into jobs can only be a part of the campaign. Even in our sophisticated economies there is still an army of the working poor. In the end, the defeat of poverty and the victory of equality have to go hand in hand. In modern society they together make up the moral imperative of social democracy.

I do not doubt that, in the long run, we all gain from the benefits that greater equality brings. They range from the economic benefit derived from living in a better educated and healthier society to the social advantage of at least ending the social disruption which comes from social alienation. But the most important reason for advocating greater equality is that it is morally right. Until we argue for it in those terms, we will never have the nerve to carry the fight to the conservative enemy.

This is not the place to deal with, and dismiss, the many bogus arguments with which equality is challenged. But one is particularly important and has a bizarre relevance to the 1909 campaign against the Poor Law. When, fifteen years ago, I wrote Labour's Statement of Aims and Values, I began with the assertion that liberty was social democracy's primary objective. That in no way diminished the importance of equality: for until a society is equal, it cannot be truly free. True freedom is not the <u>right</u> to enjoy the opportunities which democracy provides. It is the <u>ability</u> to exercise the choices which liberty provides. The absence of restraint is only the first step. The second has to be the provision of the resources that change economic as well as legal status.

For most slaves in the southern states of America, the Emancipation Declaration changed nothing. They were free to leave the plantations but, because of their poverty, they remained in virtual servitude. Of course, in depriving a rich man of ten per cent of his income we would be guilty of what Jeremy Bentham called an "infraction" of his liberty – of the freedom to spend his full earnings. But by spreading that ten per cent among a dozen poor families we would increase their freedom to enjoy what most of society regards as their natural rights. And, in consequence, the sum of freedom would be enhanced. Think of the Poor Law Amendment Act of 1834. The freedom of wealthy burghers not to finance 'outdoor relief' from their rates was preserved. But how much liberty did the paupers – incarcerated in workhouses – enjoy? Spreading the money about would have made them free or freer. Redistribution usually has that effect. Greater equality always does.

3. POVERTY AND THE WORKHOUSE

Sarah Wise

The caricatures of Dickens are well known to us, but the extent of poor law poverty – the sheer numbers in the workhouses and the circumstances that led people to be condemned there – are not. Sarah Wise shows us inside the workhouse and gives a glimpse of the true nature of the poverty and hardship that provided the background for the Royal Commission.

"The poor old Commission – and it is getting more old and weary, if not actually senile, with every week's sitting. It is floundering about in its morass of a report... Are all men quite so imbecile as that lot are?"

Beatrice Webb's typically tart diary entry for 15 December 1908 was written a fortnight before she and her three colleagues completed their Minority Report of the 1905-9 Royal Commission on the Poor Law. What was to pique her even more, in two months' time, was her realisation that the Majority Report of the Royal Commission was not, as she had originally believed, simply the 1834 New Poor Law dressed up in new robes, but – as she told her diary on 22 February 1909 – "an immense step... In a sense, the Majority Report meant success to our cause, but not victory to ourselves. That the principles of 1834 should die so easily is certainly a thoroughgoing surprise. Even *The Spectator* acquiesces."

All the more odd, then, to early 21st century minds, is Webb's striking of certain 1834 attitudes. The spirit of Malthus haunts the Minority Report (as it does the Majority Report), with talk of "the prevention of the continued procreation of the feeble-minded... Female inmates of these great establishments [workhouses] have been known to bear offspring to male inmates and thus increase the burden on the Poor Rate."

The Minority Report chapter on 'Indoor Relief' (to give the workhouse system its proper name) opens with a blasting of the General Mixed Workhouse, in which the able-bodied, the aged, children, the infirm, the acutely sick and the 'morally degenerate' lived alongside one another. This, the Minority Report stated, was a "promiscuity" that "must be injurious", with the continuous social intercourse between young and old, hardened and innocent, loafer and genuinely out-of-work.

Respectable elderly women were – the Report claimed – annoyed constantly by noisy, dirty imbeciles, while the paralytic, the epileptic, deserted wives, widows who had been refused 'outdoor relief' (cash, food, coals and so on, provided in their own homes) intermingled in buildings that were "impregnated through and through with the atmosphere of pauperism". The Report approvingly quoted the vice-chair of the Manchester Board of Guardians of the Poor: "to the reputable clean-minded inmate, this association with the depraved is the bitterest and most humiliating experience."

Worse, the Minority Report stated, the General Mixed Workhouse did not allow the targeted curative "proper treatment" of individuals that ought to be the underpinning principle of relief. (Though what the cures for indigence, idleness and dullness of mind were to be, the Report never did get round to detailing.)

Also condemned were the 'mixed official' – the husband and wife Master and Matron of the workhouse, who valiantly had to try to combine the duties of "rearing children from infancy to adolescence; treating sickness in all its forms, from phthisis to cancer, from maternity to senility; controlling the feeble-minded, the imbeciles, the epileptics and even the certified lunatics; reforming the mothers of illegitimate children; maintaining respectable deserted wives and widows, and setting to work the able-bodied of both sexes, not to mention the usual additional duty of harbouring vagrants..."

The Minority Report instead recommended highly specialised expertise for each separate type of impoverished person, with professionals selected and monitored according to nationally agreed standards. County councils were to supersede the Poor Law machinery in education and health (including lunacy), while pensioners, the able-bodied unemployed, vagrants and paupers were to be dealt with direct by new governmental bodies.

In its elegantly constructed, earnest and occasionally acidic prose, the Minority Report skewered the parsimony, amateurism and obstinate clinging to local custom that had grown around the 1834 New Poor Law, in contradiction of its precepts. The Poor Law, which was now lumping together all sorts and conditions of men (and women), had had its day, since it was treating the symptom – poverty – and not the underlying causes: old age, infancy, unemployment, illness, lunacy, 'moral imbecility'.

There were, at the time that the Royal Commission was sitting, 24,000 children under the age of 16 in the Mixed General Workhouses of England and Wales. And while the Commission (and the Webbs) had discovered no large-scale child neglect or cruelty, nevertheless the effect of workhouse life on a child's spiritual and intellectual well-being was felt to be immense. A witness from York had spoken at the Commission of the deadening effect of a huge institution on a child: "in York [workhouse], certainly, the children were dull and inert; they stood about like moulting crows, and did not seem able to employ themselves with any enthusiasm or vigour."

This deadening was noted in adults too. Clara S Edwards, matron of the Lambeth Workhouse in South London, had told the Commission that while the "rough women" in her charge became physically healthier in the workhouse - because of the regular three meals a day and a structured daily routine – they appeared to stagnate mentally, with memory-loss a particular feature.

Mrs Edwards said that the majority of her female inmates soon became "contented" with their lot in the workhouse, and lost any impulse towards establishing an independent life outside. They were not very "sharp" at the best of times, she said, and giving them stimulating brain-work would be unlikely to improve their dullness, she felt. Mrs Bernard Bosanquet, on the Commission, wondered aloud to Mrs Edwards whether the women's mental acuity could be boosted by the withholding of meals until each woman had learnt a bit of poetry off by heart. Mrs Edwards did not seem very impressed with this suggestion.

Richard Bushell, Master of the Bethnal Green Workhouse (where Mrs Bushell was matron), stated in his evidence to the Commission that the over-60s and the chronically sick were his most pitiful inmates, and that he – along with the charitable body the Brabazon Society – made a priority of finding light manufacture, handicraft or even hobbies for them, since their boredom and mental dullness increased with every week they spent in the workhouse.

Both Edwards and Bushell believed that most of the people who came into the workhouse had had the course of their lives severely changed by excessive drinking. Both admitted that they had never been able to establish what had led to an individual becoming a heavy drinker, but both had separately come to the conclusion that the appaling quality of working-class homes in urban areas was probably one major root cause. The pubs of the slums offered an alluring, warm, well-lit, convivial and relatively clean alternative to the damp, verminous one-room dwellings that the very poorest city and town dwellers called home in the late-Victorian and Edwardian eras. It is also possible that the conditions in the better-run workhouses of the early 20th century compared favourably to low-rent urban housing, if one had reached a point in life where independence and self-reliance no longer seemed to count for much.

On 1 January 1908, 798,898 people in the UK were on parish relief – of a total population of 42 million – of whom 116,463 were males in Poor Law institutions and 73,729 were women in the same. In rural districts and small towns, the majority of inmates in the Mixed General Workhouse were the old, the young, the sick, and the intellectually impaired. But in large towns and cities, it was noted that the numbers of men (and women, to a lesser extent) who had no physical reason not to be able to work and maintain themselves increased significantly.

London itself caused the biggest headache to those (ratepayers, parliamentarians, and many others) who worried about the financial cost of parish relief, as well as the 'demoralisation' and destruction of character that was believed to derive from being able to live off the public purse. The capital city had by far the highest proportion of 'indoor' poor; and of these, half were in the workhouse, and half were in infirmaries, homes, schools or asylums. London had been subject to huge crackdowns on 'out relief' and Guardians had been instructed to offer only the workhouse to the able-bodied. This had been a deeply resented policy, and in the 1880s things often threatened to turn ugly. In East London the premises of the local Boards of Guardians would see families close to starvation imploring to be able to obtain 'out relief', arguing that if they were forced into the workhouse, families would be split up and the rented home lost to them (there was a chronic shortage of accommodation throughout the district). The Guardians to a large extent in the 1880s had their hands tied by the Local Government Board's insistence that the workhouse only was to be offered, but protested to this Whitehall body – in a breathtaking misunderstanding of priorities – that local landlords suffered loss of rental income whenever a family was sent into the workhouse.

Working-men's groups formed to request to be able to do parish labour for a subsistence wage so that they could keep themselves and their families out of the workhouse; in Bethnal Green, local men argued persuasively (but ultimately unsuccessfully) that they should be paid to renovate the notoriously dilapidated (in the 1880s at least) Bethnal Green Workhouse.

In April 1886 inmates had attempted to blow up the workhouse at Well Street, Hackney, in east London; it was reported that these were men who had been asked to do the 'work test' to see whether they could be categorised as able-bodied or non-able-bodied – a request that was likely to have been highly inflammatory at a time of chronic unemployment, with hundreds of thousands of men able and willing to work but finding no jobs available.

These were the arguments and actions of the fit, able, eager-to-work but unemployed. It was estimated that in London's workhouses a not-very-large proportion of inmates were the dreaded 'able-bodied loafer' (Richard

Bushell could count just 13 regular able-bodied loafers in the Bethnal Green workhouse, which in 1908 accommodated 837 people). More prevalent were those whom observers suspected were technically able-bodied but were either unable or unwilling to function in the labour market. Can't work, or won't work?

Then, as now, this was a highly subjective categorisation, and the authors of the rival Majority Report would colourfully describe many people as ending up in the workhouse, "owing to their own loneliness and helplessness". With the elderly, many still appeared to be physically vigorous but had somehow seemed to have given up the fight: just a small percentage of the London aged poor were considered capable of managing outside the workhouse on a pension or on 'out relief', with elderly women appearing better able to function alone in their homes than elderly men.

Despite the comparatively low numbers of able-bodied inmates, London in 1908 was nevertheless found to be maintaining 15,800 more paupers than it had been in the 1880s – that hungry, troubled decade of high unemployment, bad harvests and extreme social unrest. Some observers blamed the introduction of the Workmen's Compensation Acts, from 1896, which, it was argued, had made employers less willing to employ mature men, throwing middle-aged and older males on to the scrap heap (and into the workhouse) since 'out relief' was so difficult to obtain in the capital.

There were rival explanations. It was frequently alleged in these years that there was an ever-increasing comfort and spirit of humanity in the workhouse after 1894 – the year in which the property qualification for being elected a local Guardian of the Poor was abolished, allowing greater numbers of working-class (unpropertied) men and women to sit on the nation's Boards of Guardians. Way back in 1886, when such a move had been debated, Lord Salisbury had said that allowing working men a say in Poor Law administration would be "rather like leaving the cat in charge of the cream jug". This attitude reappeared during the 1905-9 Royal Commission on the Poor Law, when the commissioners asked George Augustus Paul, Chairman of the West Ham Board of Guardians, whether the working-class members of his board (which was, in fact, the largest Poor Law Union in the nation) were able to "take a wise line" in regard to dispensing parish relief. Paul answered that he "did not know why they should not, except that their sympathies naturally tend to their own class... There might be larger numbers relieved, but the amount is not excessive." Paul added that working-class guardians were more "useful" than guardians of other kinds, in that they understood applicants' circumstances better; but under pressure Paul conceded that he could envisage them allowing "their heart to run away with their head".

The Royal Commission on the Aged Poor, which had sat from 1893 to 1895, had laid before the nation ample evidence of the harshness and unfairness of workhouse life for this class of deserving and respectable poor. It was widely believed that, along with the appointment of more working-class guardians, this swing in public sentiment had been a large contributor to a 'softening' of workhouse regimes. In 1895-6 the Local Government Board had introduced reforms that meant that the elderly could have their meals and go to bed at different times to the other inmates; the number of married-couple private rooms were to be increased for the aged; elderly people were no longer to be required to wear the workhouse uniform and were to be allowed outside the workhouse for walks. Although such improvements had been made in order to increase the comfort of one specific group, it was precisely because the workhouses were still Mixed and General that all types of resident had benefited, it was felt. Many believed that, as a result, the idea of the workhouse now held far less terror for the idle or for those who were either unwilling or unable to carve out their own destinies beyond the walls of an institution.

But this is not to say that passionate, violent even, protest against the workhouse system had come to an end. The spirit of insurrection was still alive at the time of the Royal Commission. Charles Mowbray – a tailor by trade, (highly) self-educated and formerly, in the mid-1880s, a major Anarchist agitator in the East End of London – led a delegation of several hundred men to the gates of the West Ham Workhouse, claiming to be intent on tearing down the gates and forcing the abolition of the Poor Law in the district, in favour of direct employment by the borough council. In the event, the agitation petered out, but it had given the London authorities a signal that working-men's opposition to the relief system was still strong.

The Minority and Majority Reports were both ignored, and it took two decades for Beatrice Webb to confide to her diary the glee at having been right: "exactly 20 years ago – in 1908 – we were putting the finishing touches to the Minority Report, I in a state of abject exhaustion. On New Year's Eve 1928 we were writing the last words of the epilogue of our lengthy history of the English Poor Law, recording the sentence of death passed by Parliament on the Boards of Guardians and the opening of a new era in the relations between the rich and the poor... To make history as well as to write it – or, to be modest, to have foreseen, 20 years ago, the exact stream of tendencies which would bring our proposal to fruition, is a pleasurable thought! So the old Webbs are chuckling over their chickens!"

4. AN UNJUST LAW

Jon Trickett

Jon Trickett MP unearths an example from his own constituency in West Yorkshire of the callous nature of the Poor Law – and worries that the class divisions which defined that era still persist in this.

The dominant Victorian attitude to poverty was clearly demonstrated in a verse of the well known hymn: *"The rich man in his castle,The poor man at his gate, God made them, high and lowly, And order'd their estate."*

The poor were thought of as people who were lazy and sought to avoid hard work. They were improvident, they were dissolute and wasted any income on drink and gambling. This analysis of the causes of poverty lay behind the Victorian application of the Poor Law and the ultimate sanction of the workhouse. Essentially a punitive regime, the Poor Law sought, by means of deterrent action, to change the behaviour of the poor.

The cutting edge of the Poor Law was the workhouse, whose cruelty was most sharply exposed by Charles Dickens' novels. In Oliver Twist he says that "at the very moment when a child had contrived to exist upon the smallest possible portion of the weakest possible food, it did perversely happen in eight and a half cases out of ten, either that it sickened from want and cold, or fell into the fire from neglect, or got half-smothered by accident; in any one of which cases, the miserable little being was usually summoned into another world."

Whilst Dickens provided a strong moral case against the Poor Law, the Minority Report mounted an intellectual challenge. The Webbs rejected the ideological presumption underlying the operation of the Poor Law in their times. Their proposed socialised welfare provision overcame the defects of the existing system and sought to confront directly the Victorian view that the able-bodied poor are exclusively or primarily responsible for their own poverty.

It may be thought that the Victorian analysis of the causes of poverty had long ceased to be held amongst 'civilised society'. This is not the case. The leader of the Conservative Party, David Cameron, during his visit to the Glasgow East by-election, talked once more of Britain as a 'broken society'. He sought to construct an argument that the fat and the poor are largely responsible for their own obesity and poverty:

"We talk about people being 'at risk of obesity' instead of talking about people who eat too much and take too little exercise. We talk about people being 'at risk of poverty, or social exclusion': it's as if these things – obesity, alcohol abuse, drug addiction – are purely external events like a plague or bad weather... Social problems are often the consequence of the choices that people make."

The impulse to blame the poor for their own poverty continues to this day.

The Kinsley lockout and evictions
In 1905, when the work of the Royal Commission on the Poor Law began, tumultuous events affecting the lives of

thousands of people in the small mining village of Kinsley were coming to a head. These events, in what is now my constituency, help explain the importance of both the Minority Report and the election of the first Labour MPs the following year.

The problems in Kinsley were exacerbated by the Poor Law. They were triggered by a failing and under-capitalised management of the local colliery affecting the lives of perhaps 4500 people by throwing them into extended poverty. The owners determined that the only way to proceed was to cut the cost of wages and over the years there were a number of altercations with the union. In 1901 for example there had been a dispute which was resolved when the Leeds Stipendiary magistrate had mediated between workforce and management resulting in an agreed wage. Notwithstanding their assent to pay this wage, the owners never implemented the agreement.

By 1905 matters spilled over into a protracted dispute. According to the men, the already low wage (less than that recommended by the Leeds Stipendiary) was now being cut in half. The dispute led, in July 1905, to some men withdrawing their labour and the rest being locked out for 39 months.

The Yorkshire Post described the situation and it is interesting to note the comment about the 'improvident' nature of these able-bodied poor.

"In all when the pit sets down, 1000 men will be out of work – which means roughly a population of 4500 people will be more or less affected. At present the Yorkshire Miners' Association is making an allowance of 9 shillings a week per member, with a shilling extra for each child; but when the house rents are 5 shillings a week and more, there is little left to keep a home together. Unhappily, too many miners are improvident. As one walked through the streets and lanes of Hemsworth, the 'betting paper' was to be noticed among practically every group of colliers."

This touches on the housing situation and the impossibility of the families to pay the rent. What it does not say is that most of the miners lived in houses which they rented from the company which owned the colliery.

And so began the most brutal episode in this whole story.

The company went straight to the Pontefract Magistrates Court to evict the families from their homes. And so literally hundreds of families faced the prospect, not only of having no income – and as a consequence little food or adequate clothing (reports of schoolchildren without shoes were widespread) – but also no home.

The evictions took place over several weeks and were carried out by the local police. Huge crowds assembled in solidarity each day when there were evictions. The men women and children were driven to live in tents provided by the union.

The *Wakefield Express* described one such event:

"In one house was Bob Battey, a miner who is highly respected and a well known musician...Bob is a very good performer on the concertina and his son is no mean harpist and he regaled the crowd outside with a selection of all kinds of music...For example when one of the companies of police came tramping up, whereupon Bob started playing 'See the conquering hero comes'...When Bob was noticed to be overcome by the distressfulness of the situation and began to weep, a man in the crowd shouted 'Cheer up Bob, don't be silly'. But this man's certainty was not the attitude of the majority of the bystanders and one or two spoke out very strongly, one turning to this man and saying 'thee wait till tha's bin put through it, and then tha'll know abaht it.'"

Clearly there was considerable poverty caused during the three-plus years of the lock-out and considerable amounts of coverage in the press, both local and national, focused on the effect on the children. A letter to the Board of Poor Law Guardians prior to the evictions detailed this: "the children are not only partially underfed, but are pining as you must observe from the following facts. Take a man with a family – a wife and five children. He receives 9 shillings personally and 1s. for each child, leaving 13s 6d after deductions after which, prior to purchasing food requisites, deduct rent average 5s 6d and other items and this leaves a balance of only 4s to maintain the entire family of 7 persons. We petition your Hon Board to request the Hemsworth Board of Guardians to feed the children."

If the appeal to feed the children was refused, then the adult applicants would have no choice but to apply for full Poor Law relief. This would in effect mean the whole families being treated as paupers and then committed to the workhouse. Some of the reasons which were used to refuse the applications for relief beggar belief and it is difficult even after a century not to feel outrage at the cold-hearted application of the Poor Law. For example, when the evictions first began, it was during the school holidays and the Guardians required evidence from the schools about the situation facing the children. The national rules said that the "Relief (school children) Order 1905 is limited to cases in which a special application is made... Special application is limited to an application by the managers or teachers within a public elementary school." Given that the school was closed for holidays, the Guardians refused to help alleviate child poverty because it followed that the Order could not apply since they could not confirm the existence of the children.

The fact is that the Guardians who were charged with mitigating against poverty set their faces from the start to the end of the struggle against assisting the poor.

At the centre of the Guardians' decision was their view that the miners could go back to work and were therefore voluntarily out of work; and as such ineligible for relief, and the same applied to their children. Here is a report of a typically sharp exchange at a meeting of the Poor Law Guardians:

> "Councillor Lincoln, (on behalf of the miners) heatedly: 'I contend there is no work for the men to go to. The pits were stopped, pure and simple, because they could not make them pay. The company has never asked the men to go back.'
>
> The Chairman: 'The Board has the matter in hand'
>
> Cllr Lincoln: 'It would never even have been discussed if your clerk had not mentioned the word strike in his letter'
>
> The clerk: 'I did not use the word 'strike', but only referred to strike pay'
>
> Cllr Lincoln: 'You said there was plenty of work for people to go to. They have construed it to mean that there is plenty of work and the men are on strike.'"

Scenes such as this were repeated almost every fortnight with the Guardians steadfastly refusing to help. The magistrates, the landowners, the company which owned the mine, the Guardians, the police, even significant parts of the established church stood by whilst men, women and children were left to their own devices.

"Only the poor help the poor"

But contrary to the Victorian idea that the poor are responsible for their own poverty because of moral failure, the miners throughout the three and a half years of the dispute continued to demonstrate moral strength, courage, and the virtues of hard work and enterprise. The Poor Law and the workhouse were deployed – as they were intended – in an attempt to drive the men back to work on lower pay (which the Webbs called 'sweated labour'). The truth is that affluent Britain turned its back on the poor of Kinsley and so the pauperised miners and their families had to rely on working class solidarity. The miners were well aware of this class divide: "only the poor help the poor", one told a local reporter.

One example of this solidarity was when the tent settlement was visited by members of the 'back to the land unemployed movement'. The idea was to begin to cultivate vegetables and other foodstuffs on land which was being unused at the time. This was taken up enthusiastically by hundreds of the men and their supporters at nearby Brierley Common, which even to this day is nothing but open moorland. Soon there was a large area under cultivation. But the local Lord of the Manor took action. Squire Foljambe, and the Earls of Liverpool, whose ancestry goes back beyond the Domesday Book and whose family have formed a part of the governing class in Britain for a thousand years, went to the courts in a successful bid to interdict this mass action, notwithstanding the fact that he made no use of this land, and nor have his descendants.

So how did the miners find the resources to stay out of work so long?

In the first place, the miners' union, the Yorkshire Miners Association, paid money weekly to the families, called Nipsey money, which the union gained from the subscriptions of all the men on the rest of the coalfield. The union too found a solution to the evictions by negotiating for a number of houses owned by another landlord, thereby enabling the homeless to be re-housed.

In the second place, the miners showed great enterprise and endeavour, organising choirs and bands to go out into all the surrounding towns and villages in order to gain an income.

And then there were the solidarity movements organised both by the union and also the Independent Labour Party, as well as some Christian groups. Marches, demonstrations and meetings all helped to raise money. One of the mainstays of the solidarity movement was the landlord of the local pub, the Kinsley Arms, who fed and sheltered literally dozens of the children throughout the whole period.

Conclusion: The rise of the Labour Party and the end of the Poor law

Kinsley demonstrates just how unsustainable were the intellectual underpinnings of the Victorian Poor Law system. Far from being lazy, lacking in courage, moral strength, or enterprise, the activities of the miners in Kinsley and Hemsworth exemplified all these virtues. And yet they were driven into poverty, and then spurned by the Board of Guardians.

Dickens had already mounted a ferocious moral attack on the whole system. But Orwell pointed out that Dickens' "radicalism is of the vaguest kind ... That is the difference between being a moralist and a politician. He has no constructive suggestions, not even a clear grasp of the nature of the society he is attacking, only an emotional perception that something is wrong."

The Webbs and their allies now mounted an intellectual attack on the system alongside Dickens' moral critique. But the Minority Report stands susceptible to a critique similar to that proposed about Dickens by Orwell: that the political vehicle necessary to secure the abolition of the Poor Law did not yet exist. The Webbs soon abandoned any hope that the radicals within the then dominant Liberal Party might bring about the necessary changes through parliamentary action.

Hence the crucial importance of the formation of the Parliamentary Labour Party. The limited gains which might occasionally be won – more often defeats – in industrial actions such as the one at Kinsley demonstrated that the liberation of the poor could only be won through the additional dimension of parliamentary action. In 1905 Labour did not yet have one MP, but the 1906 election resulted in the formation of the PLP under Keir Hardie's leadership.

In the previous year, Hardie had visited the Kinsley Miners and spoken to a huge meeting about the injustice of their situation, as part of the agitation amongst socialists everywhere in the run up to the election. Standing in the crowd that night was a young Kinsley miner, Gabriel Price, recently evicted along with his 72 year old mother. After the meeting, Gabriel joined the Labour Party and was active throughout the coming decades, being elected as the second Labour Member of Parliament for my constituency of Hemsworth in 1931.

Sadly Gabe Price died in 1934 and it took another decade before the PLP was large enough to secure a victory strong enough to elect Major Attlee as prime minister, with the political will finally to end the abomination of the Poor Law.

Kinsley exemplifies the injustice of a class-based society at the end of the Victorian period. But class divisions remain entrenched in Britain to this day and, as we enter into a new period of recession, the potential for injustice is still great. With the Tories returning to traditional views of poverty, can we honestly say that the moral, political and intellectual case for change has been made? Would the Gabe Prices of our time still be able to find their way into parliament to speak up for oppressed communities?

5. FROM PHILANTHROPY TO POLITICS

Dianne Hayter

Dianne Hayter argues that the politicians of today could learn much from the breadth of Beatrice Webb's roles as a diligent and committed researcher and campaigner, as it was her initial investigations into Poor Law poverty that led her to the pioneering conclusions of the Minority Report.

The poor, we have been told, are always with us. Our response, however, took a radical change in direction when we began to understand this was no God-given state, but that the way we organise our social and economic life creates winners and losers, with whole swathes of the population unable to share in the prosperity of the wider environment.

For generations, highly motivated and generous benefactors had given of their time or resources to improve the lot of the poor, or to promote the general good. Within the UK, we still acknowledge Thomas Coram, Tate, Carnegie, Wellcome, Octavia Hill and, more recently, Lord Sainsbury and Bill Gates.

However, at the turn of the twentieth century in Britain, one woman articulated and championed an alternative approach to poverty. Beatrice Potter was born – one of 9 sisters – to an upper middle class, wealthy industrial family in 1858, to a society where such women were 'destined to be wives'. Many other well-endowed and educated of her class – particularly wives and daughters – worked relentlessly to relieve the suffering of the poor, the infirm, debtors, the uneducated, the aged or the very young. Whether providing or campaigning for alternatives to prison, family planning, pensions, hospitals, baby clinics or schools, these philanthropists dedicated themselves to the relief of poverty.

However, Beatrice Webb (as she became) slowly took a different route. Being blessed with a good education, financial resources, proximity to leading thinkers such as Herbert Spencer and T.H. Huxley, and enthused by - and nearly married to - Joseph Chamberlain, she did more than describe and feel compassion for the degradations she witnessed around her. Having been introduced to social research by her cousin Charles Booth, on his Inquiry into the Life and Labour of the People of London, she began working amongst the very people whose circumstances she documented; understanding their lives and experiences as she recorded her data, signing on as a 'plain trouser hand' in the East End to gain firsthand experience of sweated labour in the tailoring trade, and working amongst the co-operators and mill workers of Lancashire.

It was arising from such work, aided and abetted by a sharp brain – and the ever helpful, devoted and brilliant Sidney – that Beatrice Webb wrote the Minority Report, which made the leap from philanthropy to politics. Poverty, for her, arose not from some shortcoming on the part of the poor, but from the system in which its victims lived. It was therefore the system, not the individual, which needed to change. And it was the responsibility of government to intervene, to prevent – not just alleviate – poverty.

Whilst from the comfort and consensus of 2009 these century-old words seem obvious, they were at the time a challenge.

Thus they were immediately discarded by the Majority on the Poor Law Commission and by wider society.

However, a movement had begun which was to prove unstoppable, and Webb took to the campaign trail to ensure her words were not stacked on a shelf but would become a reality. Her championing of the Minority Report proposals – through the creation of the National Council for the Prevention of Destitution, a campaign for the break-up of the Poor Law – was aimed at opinion formers as much as political decision-makers, as she was conscious of the need to build a consensus for radical reform. She was, after all, close to George Bernard Shaw, Williams Morris, H.G. Wells and their like who also employed writing, pamphleteering, art and drama to rally public opinion to support the call for change. Her work with the campaign involved writing for its journal, *The Crusade*, and undertaking lecture tours to promulgate the Report's proposals. She also engaged the young Clem Attlee to organise meetings and arrange speakers – though he often had to take to the stage himself when speakers failed to show.

There is no doubt that the solid research on which the Minority Report (as well as her earlier and subsequent writings) was based contributed to its impact. For the Webbs, there were no kite flying schema, no back-of-the-envelope pieces in *The Guardian*, but diligently considered and practical proposals, rooted in an understanding of the present as well as the possibility of the future. Today we hear of 'evidence-based' proposals as if this was a new concept rather than new terminology for an embedded Fabian attribute. The Webbs' other projects – the creation of the London School of Economics and the *New Statesman* – testify to their grasp of the tools of political action. Research, education and propaganda were as crucial as ideology to political change.

So Mrs Webb was a socialist, a researcher and a writer. But her gender is also an important part of why she matters. Born at a time of few expectations of women beyond family-making (which she had to do a-plenty in caring for her father), she soared to a career which remains a beacon to others. When today only 8 per cent of Vice Chancellors are women, there have only ever been 29 women to sit in a British Cabinet, and just 9 per cent of High Court Judges and 14 per cent of Council Leaders are women (Government Equalities Office 2008), how much more remarkable was it a century ago for a woman to shape, by her diligence, insights, writing and campaigning, a society's approach to welfare? And this was not her sole area of interest. She wrote 16 books or pamphlets (about the factory acts, trade unions, equal pay, co-operatives and the consumer movement, in addition to poverty and health) and another 15 with Sidney – all in addition to 4 volumes of diaries. An exceptional output for any one person, let alone a woman who herself had periods of great doubt of her own abilities aside from the low expectations of most people and decision makers around her. At the time of the Poor Law Commission, for example, she had to gird herself not "to be over-awed by great personages who would like to pooh pooh a woman who attempts to share in the control of affairs" (Beatrice Webb Diary, 15 December 1905).

There is also a love story at the heart of Beatrice Webb's achievements. The 50 year Webb partnership may be unique in their mutual support and joint enterprise, which saw two lives enriched in content and output by their conjoined status. Many high achievers draw on their partner's stamina, love or input, but few if any will enable two stars to burn within the same firmament of expertise. Reflecting in her diary nearly half a century back to their marriage in "a shabby little office of the Register of St Pancras

Workhouse – a fitting spot for the opening of our recognised partnership, dedicated to the abolition of poverty in the midst of riches" she wrote they had "been one and indivisible in work and rest, at home and abroad, in our private life and in our public career...(with) no single note of discord".

Whilst we rightly celebrate the core thesis and recommendations of the Minority Report, there are broader lessons to be drawn from Beatrice Webb's legacy for our generation of both political thinkers and activists. One cannot help but remark on how her own experience of, and work amongst, those whose condition she strove to improve was fundamental to her success. Before the start of her research and political work, she had worked for the Charity Organisation Society, and as a house-manager and rent-collector for a block of working-class flats in Docklands. Later, giving evidence in the House of Commons or briefing journalists, her solid research was imbued with the personal experience of the people she described. Today there are many political activists from the voluntary sector who share this action-research experience, their policies, commitment and energy fuelled by their daily work. But there are others whose understanding is second–hand: well-read and well-motivated political players but whose background or work has rarely exposed them to the implications of either no or inappropriate action. In the past, Labour Party members and leaders included many from trade unions who had grown up amongst those they represented, and whose family and neighbours remained in their home community. Today few either emerge from the most disadvantaged pockets of society or have spent time working with those groups, whether as social workers, teachers, health workers or in the voluntary sector. Given the success we attribute to Clem Attlee (schooled in the

East End, amongst trade unions and the unemployed, and at Toynbee Hall university settlement) as well as Beatrice Webb herself, perhaps the practicality and priority not just of their suggested remedies but of their implementation and the involvement of others in their delivery, provide a lesson for today. Similarly, her ability to change her views in light of evidence, experience and listening to others should not be underestimated – most notably over female suffrage which she first thought irrelevant but later supported. Perhaps our current politicians would benefit from similar rigour and open-mindedness. Hard work and dedication, however, were also central to her success – leaving H.G. Wells, for example, feeling "ashamed of (his) indolence and mental dissipation" (whilst also initially being "awfully afraid of Mrs Webb") (MacKenzie and MacKenzie, 1977, p323).

Beatrice Webb always saw people holistically, writing about the different parts of their lives but never forgetting that for the individual, it was one life led. Thus whilst her focus at different times might have been on women as trade unionists or mothers, co-operators or consumers, pensioners or unemployed, by specialising in no one area, she continued to champion their needs in the round, which today's departmentalism rarely achieves. She also understood the nature of a 'society' of which we are all parts, more than was articulated in her precise proposals. Underlying her approach was the philosophy of reciprocal obligations of those receiving benefits. It is interesting to note that, as early as 1948, Joan Simeon Clarke criticised the post war proposals because whilst the Minority Report "has had its main administrative proposals carried out...its philosophy [had been] neglected. In 1948 we find ourselves without that spiritual core to our social administration which would give citizens a sense of moral co-responsibility for furthering the basic purpose of the scheme...The 1946 Act has been publicised almost entirely in terms of the cash benefits to which people have a right in return for contributions paid." Is it one of Beatrice Webb's important points that we have still to learn, that the welfare state is not simply a right but part of a set of responsibilities that we all have to society? Had it been seen in those terms, might we have avoided subsequent criticisms of the welfare state in terms of scrounging off the state? And might it also have offered a response to what the Conservatives appear to be heading back to – taking welfare out of the political process and placing an increasing burden on charity and third sector organisations, as well as putting greater blame for poverty on the personal actions of people in 'broken Britain'? Beatrice Webb's understanding of the structural causes of poverty, the need for state-led responses, and of the welfare state as part of a web of responsibilities, has perhaps not been fully embedded in political culture.

The Webb legacy is not, therefore, simply of change which grew from radical and far-sighted proposals. It is also about what it teaches us about the political process: about the need for commitment, patience, evidence, consultation, education, involvement of decision-makers, campaigning and a personal investment in the causes championed. The barriers to progress were enormous: a woman as thought-leader amongst a deeply conservative prevailing culture (despite Liberal advances), the entrenchment of industrial and landed political power and a male-dominated parliament, judiciary and establishment.

Her own description of "our public career" triumphs the partnership but omits its results: a new approach to our understanding of society, its players, the centrality of fairness, and the responsibility of government to intervene to shape a better society for all. The legacy which remains is an obligation on today's Fabians to rededicate themselves to work to create the fairer society about which she wrote one hundred years ago, and about which she felt "a moral passion to reorder the world" (MacKenzie and MacKenzie, 1977, p320).

References

Caine, B. (1988), *Destined to be Wives: The Sisters of Beatrice Webb* (Oxford University Press)

Clarke, J. S. (1949), "The Break up of the Poor Law" in Cole, M. (ed), *The Webbs and their Work* (Muller)

Mackenzie, N and MacKenzie, J. (1977), *The First Fabians* (Weidenfeld and Nicolson)

6. THE WEBBS AND BEVERIDGE

Jose Harris

William Beveridge worked as a researcher for the Webbs in 1909. His 1942 report, however, overshadows their work as the pre-eminent social policy development of the twentieth century. Here Professor Jose Harris considers some of the reasons why the Webbs failed to have the same impact as their apprentice.

In historical accounts of modern social policy, the Royal Commission on the Poor Laws of 1905-09 – and in particular its famous Minority Report – has often been closely twinned with the Beveridge Plan of 1942, as one of the two most seminal public enquiries into the working of British social policy over the past hundred years. Each has been credited with inspiring a fundamental, even revolutionary, change in public attitudes towards poverty and welfare in Britain. And together they are seen as having progressively demolished the institutions and practices of the old, stigmatising, semi-feudal Poor Law and replacing it, first in 1908-11 with the lower storey, and then after 1942 with the complete edifice, of the modern, universalist, citizen-based welfare state. Needless to say there has been a good deal of myth-making and wishful-thinking about the perception of both these episodes. But – as with Magna Carta – neither of these 'myths' is so useless or so wholly untrue that any sensible person would wish to throw them away.

Nevertheless, in recent years the recollection of these two inquiries, both in popular imagination and in academic research, has followed very different paths. The Beveridge Plan has continued to be the subject of intense historical interest, not just among historians but among policy-makers, lawyers, economists, nutritionists, gender-specialists, social theorists, and many members of the wider public.

The Beveridge Report itself, with its clear and succinct style, has always been a best-seller; and its fame has been helped by the fact that it was published at an epic moment in British history, when wartime social solidarity and 'equal sacrifice' were at a premium. The papers of the Beveridge inquiry are readily accessible in the National Archives, and many people who consult them do so with the feeling that this was an integral episode in the history of the Second World War, so it is something we all know about. Moreover, although Beveridge in 1942 was advised by a civil service committee, his report was very explicitly the sole responsibility of Beveridge himself. His advisers were all clever but somewhat consensual figures, so the preparation of the report was marked by no great personal conflicts or clashes of ideology. In more recent times Beveridge's ideas have been scrutinised by many policy-experts in close and often highly critical detail; and after sixty years there have inevitably been many departures from his original scheme. But nonetheless, his plan is still widely perceived as the classic statement of certain very fundamental, broad-brush social principles – about universal coverage, full employment, family allowances, benefits in return for contributions, a national health service free at the point of delivery, and social welfare as both a 'contractual' and a 'citizen' right.

Despite their frequent twinning-together, however, historical memory of the Royal Commission on the Poor Laws is very different and much dimmer. Although only thirty-three years lay between them, the Beveridge Plan appeared at a moment when many social barriers seemed to be crumbling, whereas the Edwardian Poor Law Commission took place against the backcloth of one of the most extravagantly unequal decades in British history: a period when dire social misery co-existed with almost unimaginable aristocratic and plutocratic splendour, and whose whole way of life now seems utterly remote. The Commission itself was a much more diverse body than the Beveridge committee. Its members included not just civil servants but public dignitaries, doctors, trades unionists, churchmen, charity workers, academics and intellectuals, all with their own widely varying views on how resources should be distributed and social services organised in a modern industrial society.

Moreover, the sheer scale of the Poor Law inquiry – the size and far-reaching scope of its Majority and Minority Reports, the vastness and weight of its sixty leather-bound volumes of memoranda and minutes of evidence, the highly technical legal language of much of the Poor Law material, and the fact that personal records kept by the commissioners are scattered in many places and mostly written by hand – makes serious research into the ideas and inner workings of the Royal Commission much more difficult than for the Beveridge Plan. Scholars continue to burrow into the Commission's pages for local and historical detail, but so far as current policy-makers or the wider public are concerned, it has long been forgotten that those sixty monumental volumes ever existed. Instead, we continue to get our information about the Royal Commission mainly from one single source, which historians, journalists, politicians, and even literary critics have been dipping into for the past hundred years. This is of course the account generated in the books, diaries and personal correspondence of the Commission's most dazzling and dynamic member, the Fabian socialist Beatrice Webb, who was also the main dissentient voice on the Commission and author of the demand for a Minority Report.

Beatrice Webb's account both of the historic transition from Poor Law to Welfare State and her definition of what she saw as the fundamental prerequisites of a welfare system in any modern state, have resonated not just in history books but in ongoing debates about social policy ever since, even among people who have never heard of Mrs Webb or the Royal Commission. In all of this she was immensely aided by collaboration with her husband, Sidney Webb; indeed it is inconceivable that she would have been able to master the vast mass of technical detail involved in reform of the Poor Laws, without having had it all first pre-digested by Sidney. This is not to suggest that she was Sidney's intellectual inferior, but that – like many clever but relatively uneducated persons of her generation – she found it almost impossible to absorb either abstract ideas or complex factual data from written sources. Instead she absorbed them via Sidney, who was famed among some of the greatest legal minds in the land for his mastery of dense technical and administrative detail.

The outcome of this collaboration was a comprehensive programme for the wholesale reconstruction of social services in early twentieth-century Britain. The Webbs' programme, as it evolved over the four years of the Commission's work, included many detailed proposals relating to all the different areas of social concern covered by the existing Poor Laws (together with some that were not). But, in addition, these disparate proposals were fused together by a number of over-arching principles, each of which was framed in stark opposition to what the Webbs denounced as the sterile and self-defeating philosophy of the historic Poor Laws.

One very positive outcome of the Webbs' proposals, and of their ensuing 'campaign for the break-up of the Poor Laws', was that they galvanised what might otherwise have been a rather stuffy, legalistic, and behind-the-scenes inquiry, into a deeply ideological national debate on all aspects of the social problem, that was to last for many decades (indeed it was still ongoing three decades later, at the time of the Beveridge Plan). But there were nevertheless a number of negative consequences to the Webbs' increasingly intransigent, even messianic, Minority position. One downside was that it led Beatrice herself into a degree of prolonged estrangement from her fellow-commissioners, and of arrogant contempt for their underlying views and convictions. That some of those views were negative and backward-looking, as Beatrice claimed, was certainly true; but with others it was quite the reverse. Indeed, in their different ways, many members of the Commission (Professor William Smart, Helen Bosanquet, Dr Lancelot Phelps, Russell Wakefield, George Lansbury, Thomas Hancock Nunn, even the aristocratic chairman, Lord George Hamilton) were no less progressive and attuned to the complexities of modern industrial society than Beatrice herself. Several of them indeed were very much more alert than she was to such values as democratic self-government, the promotion of active citizenship, and the dangers of allowing administrative 'efficiency' to ride roughshod over personal liberties.

There was no real quarrel on the Commission about the need to make social services in general much more comprehensive and preventive and less stigmatic than in the past: the main policy differences between the two sides were that the Majority envisaged a much larger role for the voluntary sector; wanted to retain a specialist 'destitution' authority for social derelicts and down-and-outs; and were much more interested than the Webbs in the future prospects for new ideas about social insurance. But with these exceptions, the substance of the Minority and Majority reports when they eventually appeared was in fact remarkably similar, even though the language of the Minority was apocalyptic in tone, whereas the Majority was cautiously pragmatic.

But publication of two separate reports proved, in the long-run, a tactical mistake. As was predicted at the time by the young William Beveridge, it enabled politicians of all kinds simply to cherry-pick the two reports as they thought fit, or else simply to do nothing – a point regretfully conceded many years later by Beatrice Webb herself. (This was in marked contrast to the early-1940s, when Labour, Conservative, Liberal, and even Communist politicians, whatever their private convictions, felt bound to declare their public allegiance to the Beveridge Plan, because no alternatives were available).

There are certain puzzling aspects of the 1909 Poor Law debates, and particularly in the contribution of the Webbs.[1] One point that should be stressed is the strikingly non-Fabian character of the stance that was taken up by the Webbs over many of the issues raised by the Minority

[1] More detailed analysis of the Majority and Minority reports and their differences of emphasis lie beyond the scope of this chapter and are in any case readily available, in, for instance, the work of Professor AM MacBriar: McBriar, A. M (1987) *An Edwardian Mixed Doubles. The Bosanquets versus the Webbs* (Clarendon Press,)

Report. This point relates partly to the highly coercive and regulatory aspects of many of the policies recommended by the Minority (in striking opposition to the views of many Fabians of the Edwardian period). More particularly, however, it refers to Beatrice Webb's absolute refusal to contemplate any element of negotiation and compromise in her dealings with her fellow-commissioners. This intransigence seems to be directly at odds with the avowed Fabian philosophy of advancing reforms through reasoned persuasion and 'permeation'. All histories of the Society mention the deep divisions and prolonged crisis that occurred within the Fabian membership in 1910-12, with most accounts emphasising the tensions that arose over contested personal philosophies and individual lifestyles. The evidence of Poor Law writings, however, seems to suggest that the markedly authoritarian and coercive elements in the Webbs' 'campaign for the break-up of the Poor Laws', may have been at least as significant a factor in these temperamental divisions and debates.

Within this context, it seems plausible to speculate that, if Sidney Webb rather than Beatrice had been the main democratic-socialist representative on the Poor Law Commission, then the intellectual ambience and outcome of that inquiry might well have been very different. Indeed, if Sidney had been a commissioner, then he would undoubtedly have been far more knowledgeable than any other member (including the senior legal civil servants) about the Poor Law's day-to-day working and underlying principles. Almost certainly he would have become the chief draughtsman of the Commission's final report, thereby obviating any need for a confrontational stance between a Majority and Minority. And he might also have brought to bear a much more detached, evolutionary, and historical perspective to the embattled question of the character of the Poor Laws and the politics of poor relief, than turned out to be possible for Beatrice.

This comment may perhaps seem fanciful and counter-factual, but it is nevertheless grounded in an element of empirical fact. Twenty years earlier, before he met and married Beatrice Potter, Sidney Webb had written a most unusual and highly original essay on 'The reform of the Poor Law'. This essay had emphasised, not the negative, deterrent, and disciplinarian elements of the English Poor Law system, but its much more grass-roots, populist, and even libertarian potential within a newly-emerging democratic culture. "The poor of this country will never vote away the poor-rate", Sidney had asserted in 1890. And the English workman, he had suggested, would never submit to the kind of "regimentation, identification, and restrictions on locomotion" that was becoming common under the state-controlled social insurance and welfare schemes on the continent of Europe. Some years later, when Sidney and Beatrice were newly-married, but he was still very much the predominant partner in their common research enterprise, Sidney had been the prime author of their joint work on *Industrial Democracy* in 1898. This book had again strongly emphasised the democratic, civic, and communal significance, as well as the merely 'social welfare' aspects, of the multitude of mutual welfare schemes in the length and breadth of Great Britain. Such bodies were run by self-governing workers' organisations, lightly regulated by the common law, but were otherwise free from either government or direct employer interference. This populist and employee-based element in social welfare was almost entirely absent, however, from the 1909 Minority Report, which – as indicated above – envisaged welfare schemes of all kinds as being directly under the control of local and central bureaucracy.

A final anomaly in the Webbs' analysis of the Poor Law in 1909 was that – again in marked contrast to their earlier work on trades unionism, and also to Sidney's writings in his pre-Beatrice days – their ideas about social welfare were formulated with almost no reference to the views of the pauper client or the poor person in the street. In this neglect, however, the Webbs were no different from any other Poor Law commentators of the Edwardian age. One of the most interesting features of the 1905-09 Royal Commission was that, unusually for such a body, it did receive extensive evidence not just from the great and good, but from working men and women, including some who were or had been inmates of workhouses and recipients of outdoor relief. Reference to such evidence scarcely figured at all in either the Minority or the Majority reports, however; possibly because, in such a deeply class-based society, the opinions of working people were deemed of little or no significance. More probably, though, it was because the views expressed were in nearly all cases very remote from what either the Majority or Minority commissioners would have expected to hear. These were that, for the most part, the Edwardian Poor Law system was modestly popular with a majority of working-people in Britain; that it fitted in with and complemented the precarious irregularities of working-class life; that relieving officers were almost universally respected; and that the 'shame' attached to poor relief was greatly exaggerated by the sensitive classes.

The main popular grievance about the Poor Law appeared to be, not its excessive harshness but its laxness, in failing to weed out and segregate the small minority of paupers who were perceived by their fellow-paupers as anti-social, insanitary, and exploitative. This dimension of the Royal Commission of the Poor Laws, deeply embedded in the sixty neglected bound volumes of evidence, may or may not have been representative of wider grass-roots opinion of the period: but it deserves much more attention from historians and others than it has so far received.

7. BEYOND BEATRICE

Seema Malhotra

Beatrice Webb is the best known Fabian woman of her generation but, as Seema Malhotra argues, the role of other Fabian women in fighting poverty demands greater recognition.

"Who were the two most brilliant members of [the Royal Commission on the Poor Law]? Who were the two people who took greatest part in building up both the Majority and Minority reports? The two persons who were the most industrious and gave the most help on the Commission were Helen Bosanquet and Beatrice Webb."

Thus socialist MP, and future leader of the Labour Party, George Lansbury urged his parliamentary colleagues to support the Women's Enfranchisement Bill in 1911. He was understandably impressed by the work that had gone into the Royal Commission: after all, it would be another seventeen years before women were to vote on equal terms with men, yet two women were leading the major political debate of the time - the reform of the Poor Law.

Indeed as women they were far from alone in their public contribution. Around this time, a growing number of women were taking on roles in public life, and campaigning for radical change in the position of women and the disadvantaged in society. Often overlooked is the Fabian Women's Group – a fascinating group of women who came together in the Fabian Society and over a short period created a name for themselves as important and influential intellectuals.

The nature of the relationship between the Fabian Women's Group and Beatrice Webb – probably the Society's most famous woman - and the contribution they made to each other's work has been a source of disagreement. However the relationship was always solid, and grew stronger and more mutually supportive over time. For whilst it has been suggested by Barbara Caine that Webb was "not particularly active" in the Fabian Women's Group, and that she "rarely attended" their meetings, Ryland and Nix argue that Webb "in fact had a long and productive engagement with the Group, helped shape its research programme, [and] made a great many contributions to the organisation's maintenance and development."

One explanation for this difference is that some have been sceptical about Webb's commitment to women's emancipation, in part following her signing of the Appeal Against Women's Suffrage in 1889[1]. It is probably true to say Webb did this without much thought, being preoccupied by other issues at the time, and was something that she came to regret (Caine 1982, p34).

In the early 1890s, the women's question took on increased prominence in the Fabian Society, which had a higher proportion of female members (at almost a quarter) than other socialist groups (Beals in Nyland and Rix 1998), but lacked a clearly defined women's programme. In 1891, following a discussion in the Society on a quota system for women on the

---

[1] The Appeal, published in the magazine Nineteenth Century, advocated the extension of women's domestic role to a greater public role in the community to be supported by improvements in women's education, but was against a political role.

Society's Executive – which was opposed - the Executive Committee agreed "that a Fabian pamphlet would be produced that would detail the Society's position on women's suffrage and the demand that women be accorded the civil and political rights enjoyed by men." Harriot Stanton Blatch, later a prominent suffrage campaigner in America, and who, like Webb, worked as a researcher for Charles Booth, was asked to produce the manuscript.

Blatch struggled to achieve a consensus on a Fabian view. Divisions emerged on labour laws and other issues, a further indication of the difficulties that the reformers encountered even within the Society. Perhaps to provide a way through the problem, Beatrice Webb was invited in 1895 to give a lecture to the Society on how the Factory Acts protected women industrial workers. This lecture was subsequently published and in effect, as Nyland and Rix note, "became the Society view that gender emancipation could not be separated from class emancipation" and was a turning point for Beatrice Webb's role in the Society – "the class-plus-gender perspective which [Webb] advocated that became dominant in the Society in the 1890s ... was subsequently to characterise the Fabian Women's Group."

Little further movement took place on the gender question until Maud Pember Reeves, who had played a leading role in the campaign for women's suffrage in New Zealand, put a motion to the 1907 Annual General Meeting "to embrace equal citizenship alongside the most basic socialist issues concerning the welfare of the community". The motion was seconded by Beatrice Webb. This led to a formal commitment to women's suffrage in the Fabian 'Basis' or constitution. The amendment was initially opposed by the 'Old Gang' – Sidney Webb, George Bernard Shaw, Edward Pease and Hubert Bland - due to a fear that the Society would be vulnerable to charges of "political faddism" (Nyland and Rix

1998, p111). But the amendment passed, due to the turnout of women at the meeting. For Webb, it was an opportunity to further distance herself from her 1889 signing of the Appeal.

In March 1908, Maud Pember Reeves founded the Fabian Women's Group. This was at a time of increasing violence in the suffrage campaigns, and the work of the Poor Law Commission was well underway. Webb was involved from the start, and her influence was evident in its work on poverty as well as on social and political equality. At the April 1908 meeting, a letter from Webb was tabled where she urged that the campaign for suffrage be extended to include practical electoral work (Pugh 1984). In response, the Group set up a Citizenship Committee to see that women qualified to vote in local elections were registered. Fabian women distributed the Women's Local Government Society's pamphlets on voting qualifications and helped organise in their neighbourhoods. Pugh argues that the marked change in attitude towards women in local government owed much to the work of the Fabian Women's Group. These incremental successes were key moments on the journey to equal franchise.

That the Fabian women came together at all is partly as a consequence of earlier reforms that had allowed access for women to higher education and to roles in local public life, as well as their own organising capability and resources. Some argue that they were more active as individuals than as an organisation: it is fairer to say they did both. Through their Parliamentary Franchise campaign, group members were active in suffrage protests and demonstrations, coordinating their activities with other bodies. In 1908, eleven members were also jailed. There is no doubt the impact of what they did as individuals was strengthened by being part of a coordinating network for change.

Sally Alexander expounds the view that without the work of the Fabian women, the movements for economic and political equality would not have been likely to gain the momentum they did. She particularly highlights the impact of the Group's first book, which included Webb's explanations of women's low pay and arguments for factory legislation, Pember Reeves' research on life in Lambeth on a pound a week, Barbara Hutchins's coverage of the different economic needs of women at different phases in their lives and Barbara Drake's study of women and trade unions.

Fabian women were also a voice for reform on a wider range of equality issues. For example, Ethel Bentham gave evidence to the Royal Commission on Divorce expressing the views of the Fabian Women's Group who had met to discuss the issues at the home of Mrs Ramsey MacDonald with other women's organisations.

The Group helped the women's movement more through empirical research than activism. Although their work was often obscured by their more famous contemporaries such as Booth and Rowntree, Howard Glennerster points out that "much of [the Group's] work was qualitative and it explored the meaning and experience of poverty for individual family members and notably women. It was influential because it gave an accessible parallel account to that of Rowntree…It also raised issues about the distribution of income within families that feminists were to rediscover in the 1980s" (Glennerster et al 2004, p27).

Webb enlisted the support of the Fabian Women's Group to continue the campaign for change following publication of the Minority Report. They promoted the report's findings, gave lectures and engaged with the National Committee for the Promotion of the Break-Up of the Poor Law at the request of Webb. These campaigns, seen increasingly through the lens of gender, were critical to ensuring the Minority Report was not an 'island', but instead became an anchor in a wider movement for class and gender equality, committed to tackling poverty more humanely, rewarding women for their labour more fairly and building the arguments in new ways for greater women's representation.

That the Fabian Society itself had such a critical mass of educated and committed women is a testament to the environment the early Fabians created. To some extent the Fabian women were overshadowed by the men, and – apart from Webb – the work of the other Fabian women is rarely referred to. But Fabian women increased the focus on class and gender issues relating to poverty, and directly contributed to a sea change in attitude towards the power and necessity of social investigation and evidence based social policy. They could have gone further had the men been less resistant, but considering the stage of public debate and the legacy they inherited of wider Victorian social attitudes and structures, it is a testament to their passion for change and their courage that they were able to achieve as much as they did.

References

Alexander, S. (1979), *Introduction to Maud Pember Reeves, Round About a Pound a Week* (London)

Caine, B. (1982), *Beatrice Webb and the Woman Question* (History Workshop Journal)

Glennerster H. et al (2004) *One Hundred Years of Poverty and Policy* (Joseph Rowntree Foundation)

Nyland, C. and Rix, M. (1998), 'Beatrice Webb and the Fabian Women's Group' in Beilharz, P. and Nyland, C. (ed) *The Webbs, Fabianism and Feminism: Fabianism and the Political Economy of Everyday Life* (Ashgate)

8. IN PRAISE OF THE MAJORITY REPORT

Nick Bosanquet

The welfare state, born out of the political conflicts of the twentieth century, now seems likely to decline in the economic turbulence of the twenty first, says Nick Bosanquet; and he finds that it is the Majority Report that offers the more compelling direction for the future.

The Poor Law Commission of 1909 was not a landmark but the end of a road. The Majority and Minority Reports had common origins in nineteenth century thinking and concepts. They were both written from a common basis of idealism. The aim was individual self-improvement within a society which was seen as an organism of civil groups.

The key focus was on social improvement not on social engineering. In this light the Majority Report looks a great deal better documented and argued than the Minority Report. Helen Bosanquet – a cousin of mine by marriage – was the leading spirit. She was not the fearsome anachronism of social policy myth. She was in fact more part of the social policy establishment of the time than Beatrice Webb and they were both associated with the LSE, where Bosanquet taught some of the first courses in social work.

The Bosanquet Majority plan was for the development of specific services for specific groups. Thus for older people she was in favour of sheltered housing. For children she advocated improvement in conditions and the extension of fostering. And for people of working age she wanted something like a welfare-to-work scheme. In fact at times she seemed more sympathetic to the poor – and indeed rather less judgmental of them – than Beatrice Webb, with her plans for labour colonies in East Anglia and her search for undeserving characters among the aged poor.

Winston Churchill was not alone in not wanting to be shut up in a soup kitchen with Mrs Sidney Webb – it was the whole British establishment. It took the Great War, the new electorate and the powerful concept of the 'national minimum' (with Sidney Webb very much in the lead on this) to bring the Webbs and their ideas to power. In fact the Majority Report represented the eclipse of Mrs Webb, who suffered a nervous collapse after Helen Bosanquet exposed her manipulation of data from a survey of Workhouse Medical Officers (Radice, 1984). Helen Bosanquet may not have changed history but she certainly changed the Webbs. In fact, although not formally implemented, it was the approach of the Majority Report which became the model for British social policy. The lack of reform of the Poor Law left room for many new services to develop which might well not have developed if a new and costly national bureaucracy had followed from the Minority Report. Notable especially were the maternity clinics and child welfare centres started by Sylvia Pankhurst and others.

The Poor Law Commission, appointed in the last phase of the Conservative Balfour Government, was not in touch with the emergence of the new Liberalism led by Lloyd George and Churchill, which improved a range of insurance schemes to add up to the new 'national minimum'. Nor did it have much of the increasing success of local government in its public health role. The Poor Law Commission saw social policies as applying to people on the fringe of society who had been excluded from the general population by age, misfortune or lack of moral fibre. It was the last gasp of arguments left over from the nineteenth century rather than the construction of Lloyd George's new 'ambulance wagon' – the metaphor he used in 1911 for the caring role of the state. Notable was the strong opposition of the Webbs to the use of insurance and their role as the leading critics of the National Health Insurance Act.

In fact the ambulance wagon proved outstandingly effective. The main success in the century after the Poor Law Commission report was the combination of insurance and increased role for local government after 1906, not the post-1945 Beveridge welfare state. In 1871 life expectancy at birth was around 41 – much the same as it had been in 1571. This was mainly the result of very high infant and child mortality: even in that period an individual who survived into adulthood had a good chance of living into their 20s. From 1871 on there was a rise in life expectancy which accelerated after 1901 so that by 1939 life expectancy at birth was around 65. There was a very big improvement for infant mortality – from 180 per 1000 to 30 – and also in adult health and height. We hear a lot from social policy texts about how 40 per cent of the recruits for the South African war in 1899 were rejected as unfit, but rather less about the fact that only 2.7 per cent of the recruits in 1939 were rejected as unfit (Macleod, 1962).

The ambulance wagon may have been socially effective but it was not politically conclusive. The system was complex with many anomalies as it was made up of specific benefits for specific groups. Following a war that led to powerful pressure for change and reconstruction, Beveridge promised order and consistency around the grand aim of security for all in the land, rather than the Poor Law Reports' more modest focus on the subsistence of a minority.

The main success of the post-1945 welfare state was in reducing poverty in old age. At the time of the Beveridge Report it was expected that the ageing population would be a burden which would weigh down on a diminishing number of younger tax payers. In the event the policy mix worked well and by 2005 older people had seen a distinctive rise in living standards: but the reasons for this success were as much due to private/public partnership as to the level of state benefits. This success was brought about by a combination of voluntary effort with state benefits: but without the voluntary effort the position would have been much worse.

The NHS certainly generated a sense of security and in the first ten years created a national chain of hospital services which had never existed before, but there was nothing exceptional about the outcomes achieved in the long term. A free service could have been delivered in different and better ways than a centralised monopoly, which was too big to fail and also too big to manage effectively. There were many opportunities then – and there still are now – to empower more local initiative.

The NHS development was one part of a wider problem – that of increased centralisation. Here the Webbs may have had influence in the long-term movement towards centrally managed programmes which has been such a distinctive feature of the British scene since 1945. UK national governments have shown a deep suspicion of local government and have now left it in many areas with a multi-tier structure which more or less ensures confusion and ineffectiveness. In 1935 a cross party group proudly published *A Century of Municipal Progress 1835 to 1935* (Laski 1935). It recorded real and important gains in education, housing and public health. It is hardly likely that a similar exercise will be credible in 2035. The missed opportunity was the City Region concept which would have meant the UK had around 70 single-tier authorities based on counties and city regions. It may be, however, that devolution in the UK will bring about some greater pressure for change given that Whitehall now only rules England - not Scotland and Wales.

For me it was partly the experience of the housing choices and standards promoted by decades of heavy investment in council housing which shifted me - in eight years a as a councillor in an inner city ward – towards more personal and market-based solutions. Having been an active Fabian and Chair of the Society in 1973-4, I found that I could no longer share the Fabian optimism about the benefits of state activity. I was also influenced by contact with the then NHS monopoly services for people with learning disability, which showed the abysmal failure of centralised monopoly. A very few of us made the case in the 1970s for more choice and a greater role for parents and carers: this has actually happened and has brought about a great improvement in care.

All the main members of the Majority and Minority would have been incredulous about the fact that one fifth of the working age adult population in 2007 was out of the workforce and supported by benefits. That there are still communities where a third of the population are dependent on welfare would have been unfathomable to them. Both Helen Bosanquet and Beatrice Webb were very concerned about the issue of work incentives and would have welcomed the new initiatives to increase them. In fact the 2009 approach proposed in James Purnell's Welfare Reform Bill is quite close to the individual interviews which Helen Bosanquet developed for the Charity Organisation Society.

Thus we find ourselves at the beginning of the twenty first century with social policy moving back to the same issues of individual initiative which were all too familiar in the nineteenth century. Personal motivation and ownership are becoming more discussed in a number of different areas. The state pension is to be set at a minimum, with individual savings accounts providing most of income in retirement. Disability benefits are to be subject to a test of ability and readiness to work. Education is to be entrusted to independent city academies. And even the NHS is moving towards personal health plans patient choice, individual budgets and top up payments.

At the centenary of the Poor Law Commission, it is the values of the Majority Report which seem to be attracting renewed interest: the twentieth century welfare state based on state monopoly and automatic entitlement seems likely to be replaced by a system which lays more emphasis on personal capability and local initiative. Many Fabians have yet to face up to the fact that more responsibility and choice for individuals must mean that they have more of their own money to spend. Fabians, along with many on the left, seem to see the level of taxation which bought the welfare state safety net as appropriate to a situation in which personal savings and personal debts put much more pressure on individuals to pay for their own support in old age and to pay off fees for higher education. Fabians now need to tell us what they think is the appropriate tax-and-spend balance for the post-Webb conditions of the twenty first century.

References

Laski, H. (ed). (1978 [1935]), *A Century of Municipal Progress 1835-1935* (Greenwood Press)

Longmate, N. (1974), *The Workhouse* (Maurice Temple Smith, London)

Macleod, I. (1962), *Neville Chamberlain* (Muller)

Radice, L. (1984), *Beatrice and Sidney Webb* (Macmillan)

9. THE 2009 MINORITY REPORT ON THE WORLD BANK

Peter Townsend

What would the Webbs do in 2009? In this article, Professor Peter Townsend adopts the Webbs' authoritative style of planning and applies some of the precepts they used to challenge the domestic poverty of the failed Poor Laws in 1909 to the global poverty that faces us today.

In present conditions I believe the Webbs would see that 2009 offers an extraordinary opportunity to re-establish some of the values expressed in 1909 in relation to new policies. I am thinking in particular of human rights and John Maynard Keynes. Today the problem is not just regulation or reconstruction of banks – but of other global institutions, and particularly the World Bank.

The World Bank has failed to diminish poverty in the developing world. That failure is surely a contributory factor in the unprecedented 2008 collapse of the global financial system. Getting rich quick has meant exploiting many millions on the lowest incomes and failing to satisfy their basic human rights. And this can be ascribed to the reach and dominance of neo-liberal economic ideology in the last 40 years.

This ideology germinated in 1944 with Hayek's *Road to Serfdom*. Despite being treated for decades as an arch conservative whose views could not be taken seriously, and despite the postures of organisations created in his name, like the Institute for Economic Affairs in the UK in the 1950s and 1960s, his free market position was given a shot in the arm by the Chicago School of economists and in particular by Milton Friedman.

Monetarism gained adherents and prospered. The objective of a free global market gathered momentum. The collapse of the Soviet Union and the protracted period of power exercised by the Republican Party in the United States through the election triumphs of Nixon, Reagan, Bush senior and Bush junior gave a fillip to neo-liberal economic policies. This led inevitably to the stark inequalities produced by public expenditure cuts, privatisation, smaller and less progressive taxes, anti-union legislation, and free trade in the interests of western-based global corporations.

The World Bank has served its masters dutifully and effectively. Its influence is all-pervasive. But lingering extreme poverty on a huge scale and realisation of the deep faults in the banking system invites an urgent review of the Bank's work.

The failure to advise effectively about world poverty is the most compelling example.

Since 2000 the primary goal of the United Nations to halve world poverty by 2015 has been at odds with the reality of unremitting social polarisation and degrading mass poverty. There have been a growing number of reports reliably documenting both. The World Bank has nonetheless persisted with its discriminatory measure of poverty and its selective and unsuccessful policies.

Measurement Failures

For many years the World Bank made claims of a steady decline in the scale of poverty. But gradually the decline – even on the Bank's figures – looked slow and halting and the

Bank's technical expertise was convincingly questioned. Economists have savaged the technical updating of the dollar-a-day poverty line from year to year, and the way that poverty line was translated into the equivalent purchasing power in the currency of each particular country. Thus, Kakwani and Son (2006) show that if the poverty line up to 2005 had been pitched at a level of $1.50 instead of $1.08 in the mid and late 1990s to allow for the true, and properly weighted, levels of inflation around the world, the count of those in severe poverty would have been much larger. Absolute poverty in the world would have been 36 per cent and not 21 per cent in 2001 – raising the total numbers by 800 millions to little short of 2 billions.

The second measurement fault is more fundamental. The Bank's practice since 1985 has been to restrict the measure of a 'poverty line' to material needs and not include social needs – such as people's needs to meet the costs of going to work and their obligations to family and society. In the early 1990s the Bank stated repeatedly that these were the two necessary elements in the measure of poverty (World Bank, 1990, p.26; and see also World Bank, 1993a, 1993b, 1996, 1997, 2000, and 2001). By the World Bank's own authority, the scale of world poverty must have been routinely under-estimated ever since.

For half a century the Bank has obstructed the development of a measure of poverty that is international and scientific. The UN initiative at the Copenhagen World Summit in 1995 – which would have begun to allow rich and poor countries to be compared – was ignored. In 2008 two researchers at the Bank stated that "richer countries tend to adopt higher standards of living in defining poverty" and that the Bank has "aimed to apply a common (sic) standard, anchored to what poverty means in the world's poorest countries." (Chen and Ravallion, 2008, p.2)

The measure is circular as well as discriminatory. Current very low income is treated as equivalent to minimum income need. But how can the choice of a threshold of poverty or a poverty 'line' be validated? In principle the scientific approach would be to choose criteria other than income to examine in order to provide acceptable evidence of a threshold of income that satisfies need. One such alternative is the collection of representative household information about multiple material and social deprivation. An appendix gives an example of the use that can be made of existing cross-national surveys to derive reliable indicators.

The World Bank authors finally admitted in 2008 that the celebration of the apparently sharp decline in poverty that the Bank claimed again and again in the 1990s and early 2000s had been "premature": the results had been biased and based on "rather crude price surveys" for just 10 countries (ibid, p.3). The quantity but not quality of items had been priced. Poverty in China was underestimated, they say, by 300 millions.

But old habits die hard. For the World Bank's researchers to admit some necessary technical adjustments, and accept minor retrospective adjustments in the figures they had published in the past is not the same as admitting the big mistakes that had been made for decades in Bank methodology. They have failed to establish a reliable basis for measuring trends in poverty in developing countries that genuinely allows for inflation. Thus, the researchers do not discuss what inflation index applies best to developing countries. They do not withdraw the $1.08 figure for inflation between 1985 and 1993 of a poverty line of $1.00 per person per day in 1985 in favour of the more appropriate $1.50 testified by critics. And this refusal of course affects the choice of the figure for 2005. The World Bank's spokesmen say the "new international poverty line" for 2005 follows "the same definition used in our past work, namely that the line should be representative of the national lines found in the poorest countries" (ibid, pp 3, 9-10). But arbitrary choice of the number of countries and arbitrary selection of a threshold of income is not selection according to pecuniary need.

World Bank Policies

Along with the UN and all international organisations, the Bank has upheld economic growth, debt relief and overseas aid as the primary instruments of global anti-poverty strategy. More recently fairer trade, through reform of the WTO, has been added. But different policies on behalf of these four objectives have not been examined closely to reveal what are the specific effects of each of them on the scale and distribution of continuing poverty. Policies developed in their name are relatively indiscriminate and poorly designed in their distributional effect upon population poverty. Without detailed evidence of policy delivery these strategies can be regarded only as empty shells. Success depends on whether a sufficient share of additional cash income and income in kind from these sources happens to reach the poor, and quickly. Their intentions are not always clear and their consequences left uncharted. The blithe assumption that they are good in themselves has not yet been replaced with resolute determination to ensure that policies in their name are pro-poor.

From the 1980s the World Bank has followed a three-fold strategy to reduce poverty: broad-based economic growth; development of human capital through education; and safety-nets for vulnerable groups. But investment in children's education can only begin to have an effect on the poverty rate years later, if at all, when the children become working adults – while the dire effects of poverty are ever-present. And 'safety-nets' that comprise concessions for the extreme poor through selective policies disguise the tiny scale of the commitment of resources to these policies and therefore to a problem that in many countries affects the majority of the population.

The Bank has not contributed much to the diminution of extreme poverty. In 2005 it lent approximately $22 billion but only $2.4 billion (10 per cent) was for social protection (Hall, 2007). The largest lending was for financial and private sector development and two other large allocations for urban development and environmental and natural resource management – these three making up half the Bank's programme. The sum for social protection is less than five-hundredths of one per cent of world GDP and is dwarfed by the sum spent each year by each of the rich countries on social protection (or social security) alone. Thus, the UK Department of Work and Pensions spent the equivalent of $210 billion in 2005, compared with the World Bank's total loans for social protection in the entire world of $2.4 billion.

The latest news carries an even worse indictment. In 2008 the Bank committed less than half of what it had committed in 2005 to social protection – 4 per cent of the total of $24.7 billion in the year – i.e. $0.9 billion, compared with $2.4 billion in 2005 (World Bank, 2008b).

The Bank's action remains deliberately puny and has done little to change the entrenchment of free market policies: one analyst concluded that social policy had been condemned to a "residual category of safety nets" (Tendler, 2004, p.119).

Yet as much as two-thirds of the poverty that would otherwise exist in the rich countries has been ruled out by the development of their social security systems. While public expenditure on social protection, more properly named social security (such as on child benefit, sickness and disability benefit and pensions for the elderly) has continued to increase (nearly 14 per cent of GDP in 2005) in the average OECD country, it is between 1 per cent and 3 per cent in most low income countries: for example, 1.5 per cent in India (Townsend, 2007, p.9, and see also ILO, 2001). Because the redistributive mechanisms of social security are not in place, even for groups who cannot be expected to gain earnings through employment, there cannot be effective 'trickle-down' from economic growth.

Overseas aid for the extreme poor in the developing countries is also miserly. The total of all the Bank's lending throughout the world each year has reached $25 billion (World Bank, 2008a, 2008b) – less than half the average annual income of each of the biggest 500 global corporations (Fortune Magazine, 2008). At the top Wal-Mart has annual revenue of $379 billion and Exxon Mobil $373 billion - each of them 15 times greater than the World Bank's total lending. The Bank's lending represents less than 1 per cent of the annual income of the top 500 global corporations.

The Bank has done a far better job in concealing its deterrent 'poor law' policies and the relatively puny scale of resources committed than those who concocted or sought to implement the 1834 Poor Law Act. The Webbs of 1909 would be rising up in fury.

The World Bank and Keynesian Post-War Recovery

What would have been the alternative, successful, strategy for the World Bank to pursue during the last three decades? It would have been drawn from a different theory of economic and social development than that of the Chicago School of monetarism and then of neo-liberalism. Keynes argued for a kind of world central bank or 'Clearing Union' that created a deposit of new currency for every country in the world which it could count on at times of difficulty to pay creditor governments. The big countries would create a giant fund from which countries in demonstrable financial adversity could draw – up to a sizeable minimum level – without strings. Up to that minimum level they would not have to justify their policies. His was a successful precedent during the eerily similar depression years of the 1930s and the years anticipating post-war reconstruction. He believed too in the creation of jobs rather than market incentives and the protection of the unemployed and other poor by social security. His say-so was a factor lurking behind the promulgation and acceptance of the Beveridge Report – which spurred different countries into acts of redistribution of a major kind. His strategy deserves fresh examination.

After 1944 the Bretton Woods institutions turned out to be a pale shadow of Keynes' intentions. Total resources provided for them were less than a third of what he advised. Countries were not awarded an allocation. They had to contribute to the total Fund to be eligible for membership and hence have the opportunity to apply for loans – to which stringent conditions could be attached. Membership was conditional rather than universal; debtors had less independence, aid had strings, and the US remained predominantly in charge of those strings.

In the pages above the desolate outcome has been sketched. The consequences of neo-liberal economic thought are to be found everywhere. "Behind [the World Bank] are the economic strategies of the G8 nations and the virtually unaccountable multinational corporations. The Bank is not a humanitarian agency and its analysts usually evaluate its operations on the economic principle of efficiency. Yet growing inequality is literally a matter of life and death to many millions of people" (Turshen, p.131).

Transformation of the World Bank

The World Bank has helped to implant neo-liberal ideology among governments, corporations and consumers, weakened the state and reinforced economic inequality and gross destitution. In 2009 its resonance has a hollow ring. As a vehicle with capacity to influence organisations world-wide by employing a large number of internationally informed and intelligent people, it has been driven by the wrong forces subservient to that neo-liberal philosophy. It advocates disastrous policies, lends with discriminatory conditions, and has little experience or resources to invest grants directly in jobs, services and people.

Altogether it has the wrong policies and ignores human rights.

Action has to be governed by motives of job creation, public service, staged international planning, accountable leadership, and collective organisation of social security and other social services.

The largest global corporations and international agencies (including the banks and insurance corporations, which in 2006-7 made up 100 of the 500 largest corporations) would attract praise by committing a very small percentage of their growing resources to social security and a larger percentage to minimum rights to wages and employment conditions in the low income countries. That would mean keeping track of activities in subsidiaries and sub-contracted employment, and extending rights to those workers. New international company law (Townsend and Gordon, 2002), and more effective international taxation, would be necessary components. 'Corporate social responsibility' would thereby acquire meaning.

For example global corporations could add one or two per cent of wage costs in different countries towards a universal child benefit to help banish malnutrition, poverty and premature child death, and also encourage more schooling and access to health care. Employer contributions towards domestic social insurance schemes in the OECD countries could be extended to employer operations in the low-income countries.

The creation of jobs locally and nationally would be paramount, building on some positive policies of present government. By singling out green forms of energy replacement, subsidies for domestic manufacture and farming, and expansion of some of the primary social services, the lines of an employment strategy less dependent on imports would be evident.

The strategy offers the possibility of satisfying the principal UN millennium goal of eliminating poverty, and slowing or halting runaway social polarisation; a start in the necessary reconciliation of market globalisation and public ownership and control; a principled series of stages in the fulfilment of human rights; and a feasible way of properly internationalising development.

Developing a Multiple Deprivation Index to Correlate with Household Income
(Basis of report to UNICEF 2003)

<u>Severe Food Deprivation</u> – children whose heights and weights for their age were more than three Standard Deviations below the median of the international reference population that is, severe anthropometric failure.

<u>Severe Water Deprivation</u> - children who only had access to surface water (e.g. rivers) for drinking or who lived in households where the nearest source of water was more than 15 minutes away (indicators of deprivation of water quality or quantity).

<u>Severe Deprivation of Sanitation Facilities</u> – children with no access to a toilet of any kind in the vicinity of their dwelling, - no private or communal toilets or latrines.

<u>Severe Health Deprivation</u> – children who had not been immunised against any diseases or young children who had a recent illness involving diarrhoea and had not received any medical advice or treatment.

<u>Severe Shelter Deprivation</u> – children in dwellings with more than five people per room (severe overcrowding) or with no flooring material (e.g. a mud floor).

<u>Severe Education Deprivation</u> – children aged between 7 and 18 who had never been to school and not currently attending school (no prof.l education of any kind).

<u>Severe Information Deprivation</u> – children aged between 3 and 18 with no access to, radio, television, telephone or newspapers at home.

<u>Severe Deprivation of Access to Basic Services</u> – children living 20 kilometres or more from any type of school or 50 kilometres or more from any medical facility with doctors. Unfortunately, this kind of information was only available for a few countries so it has not been possible to construct accurate regional estimates of severe deprivation of access to basic services.

Source of data on global deprivation: Demographic Health Surveys (DHS) and Multiple Indicator Cluster Surveys (MICS-UNICEF)

References

Atkinson, A.B. (1995), "Is the Welfare State Necessarily an Obstacle to Economic Growth?" *European Economic Review*, 39, pp. 46–96.

Chen, S. and Ravallion M., (2008), *The Developing World is Poorer than we Thought, but no Less Successful in The Fight Against Poverty*, Policy Research Working Paper 4703, (World Bank)

Cichon, M. and Scholz, W. et al (2004), *Financing Social Protection* (ILO, Geneva)

Donkor, K. (2002), 'Structural Adjustment and Mass Poverty in Ghana', in Townsend, P. and Gordon, D., eds. *World Poverty: New Policies to Defeat an Old Enemy* (Bristol: Policy Press)

George V. and Wilding P. (2002), *Globalisation and Human Welfare* (Palgrave)

Gordon, D, Nandy, S, Pantazis, C, Pemberton, S and Townsend, P. (2003), *Child Poverty in the Developing World* (Bristol: Policy Press)

Hall, A. (2007), "Social Policies in the World Bank" *Global Social Policy*, 7, 2.

Husain, I. and Faruqee, R. (1994), *Adjustment in Africa: Lessons from Country Case Studies, World Bank Regional and Sectoral Studies* (Washington D.C.: World Bank)

International Labour Organisation (ILO) (2001), *Social Security: A New Consensus* (Geneva: ILO)

Kakwani, N., Khandker S. and Son H. H. (2004) *Pro-Poor Growth. Concepts and Measurement with Country Case Studies*, Working Paper No. 1 (Brasilia, UNDP, International Poverty Centre)

Kakwani, N. and Son, H.H. (2006), *New Global Poverty Counts*, Working Paper Number 20 (Brasilia, UNDP, International Poverty Centre)

Mkandawire, T. ed. (2004), *Social Policy in a Development Context*, UNRISD, Basingstoke (Palgrave Macmillan)

Pogge, T. and Reddy, S. (2003), *Unknown: The Extent, Distribution and Trend of Global Income Poverty* (www.socialanalysis.org)

Ravallion, M. (2008), *Global Poverty Re-assessed: A Reply to Reddy*, One Pager, (Brasilia, International Poverty Centre)

Reddy, S.G (September 2008), *The New Global Poverty Estimates – Digging Deeper into a Hole*, One pager, (Brasilia, International Poverty Centre)

Reddy, S.G. and Pogge, T. (forthcoming) "How Not to Count the Poor," in Stiglitz J., Anand S. and Segal P. eds., *Debates on the Measurement of Global Poverty* (Oxford University Press)

Reddy, S.G. and Pogge, T.W. (2001), *"How Not to Count the Poor,"* (Departments of Economics and Philosophy, University of Columbia)

Sachs, J. (2005), *The End of Poverty* (London, Penguin Books)

Tendler, J. (2004), 'Why Social Policy is Condemned to a Residual Category of Safety Nets and What to Do About it', in Mkandawire, T. ed., *Social Policy in a Development Context,* UNRISD, (Basingstoke, Palgrave Macmillan)

Townsend, P. and Gordon, D. (2002), *World Poverty: New Policies to Defeat an Old Enemy,* especially chapters 14 and 17 (Bristol, Policy Press)

Townsend P. (2004), "From Universalism to Safety Nets: The Rise and Fall of Keynesian Influence on Social Development Policies," in Mkandawire T. ed. *Social Policy in a Development Context*, UNRISD, (Geneva, the Palgrave Press)

Turshen, M. (1999) *Privatising Health Services in Africa* (Rutgers University Press)

United Nations. (1995), *The Copenhagen Declaration and Programme of Action: The World Summit for Social Development 6–12 March 1995* (New York, United Nations Department of Publications)

World Bank. (1990), *World Development Report 1990: Poverty* (Washington, World Bank)

World Bank. (1993a), *Implementing the World Bank's Strategy to Reduce Poverty: Progress and Challenges* (Washington, World Bank)

World Bank. (1995a), *Advancing Social Development: a World Bank contribution to the Social Summit* (Washington DC, World Bank)

World Bank. (1995b), *Investing in People: the World Bank in Action* (Washington DC, World Bank)

World Bank. (1993a), *Implementing the World Bank's Strategy to Reduce Poverty: Progress and Challenges* (Washington, World Bank)

World Bank. (1993b), *World Development Report 1993: Investing in Health*, Washington, (Oxford University Press for the World Bank)

World Bank. (1996), *Poverty Reduction and the World Bank: Progress and Challenges in the 1990s* (Washington DC, World Bank)

World Bank. (1997), *Poverty Reduction and the World Bank: Progress in Fiscal 1996 and 1997* (Washington DC, World Bank)

World Bank. (1997), *The State in a Changing World: World Development Report 1997* (Washington DC, World Bank)

World Bank. (2000a), *World Development Indicators* (Washington D.C., World Bank)

World Bank. (2000b), *"Emerging Directions for a Social Protection Sector Strategy: From Safety Net to Spring Board"*, Social Protection Sector, (Washington D.C., World Bank)

World Bank. (2000), *Balancing Protection and Opportunity: A Strategy for Social Protection in the Transition Economies* (Washington D.C.,World Bank)

World Bank. (2001), *World Development Report 2000/2001: Attacking Poverty* (Washington D.C., World Bank)

World Bank. (2005), *World Bank Development Report for 2005* (Washington D.C., World Bank)

World Bank. (2008a), *World Development Report 2008* (Washington D.C., World Bank)

World Bank. (2008b), *Annual Report* (Washington D.C., World Bank)

FABIAN SOCIETY   Webb Memorial Trust

From the Workhouse to Welfare

What Beatrice Webb's 1909 Minority
Report can teach us today

A CENTENARY COLLECTION

Nick Bosanquet, Jose Harris,
Roy Hattersley, Dianne Hayter, Tim Horton,
Sunder Katwala, Seema Malhotra, Peter Townsend,
Jon Trickett, and Sarah Wise.

Discussion Guide: From the Workhouse to Welfare

How to use this Discussion Guide

The guide can be used in various ways by Fabian Local Societies, local political party meetings and trade union branches, student societies, NGOs and other groups.

■ You might hold a discussion among local members or invite a guest speaker – for example, an MP, academic or local practitioner to lead a group discussion.

■ Four different key themes are suggested. You might choose to spend 15 – 20 minutes on each area, or decide to focus the whole discussion on one of the issues for a more detailed discussion.

A discussion could address some or all of the following questions:

The 1909 Minority Report helped pave the way for the Beveridge settlement and still provides the starting point for many arguments which are central to the debates between the political parties of today. There are also lessons from the early 20th century about building the coalitions and alliances to win public arguments and make progressive change possible.

1. History and the left

- Does the left pay too little or too much attention to what its history could tell us about politics today?
- Would recovering the political traditions of the early 20th century left be useful for 21st century progressives, and if so how? Or is this era now too remote from us to be useful?
- Some people have suggested the left needs a break from the Webb tradition; others a revitalisation of it. What do we take from the Webbs now, and how relevant is the debate between the Webbs and other parts of the Fabian left tradition?

2. The role of the state

- The 1909 Minority Report and the Beveridge Report made the central case for collective responsibility and established universal welfare provision. Today there are debates about the role of the state: does the left need to take a different view on what the state should do?

- Could the left have a less statist approach that still incorporated the core insights of 1909 and what would this look like?
- What is the essential role of the state and where should the state be seen as one possible means among many?

3. The future of progressive campaigning

- What can the left learn from its success in abolishing the workhouse that could be applied to abolishing poverty today?
- Should the lessons from 1909 be as much about the campaign to abolish the Poor Law that followed the Government's rejection of the Minority Report, and the creation of new institutions such as the LSE and the New Statesman, as its actual proposals?
- The achievements of Beatrice Webb are all the more astonishing given the position of women at the time. Is there a case for seeing 1909 primarily through the lens of gender? Are there specific lessons for feminism today, and if so what are they?

Please let us know what you think

Whatever view you take of the issues, we would very much like to hear about your discussion. Please send us a summary of your debate (perhaps 300 words) to debate@fabians.org.uk. We would like to publish comments alongside the discussion guide at www.fabians.org.uk and in the Fabian Review.

Join Britain's only membership-based think tank

Join the Fabian Society and receive a free copy of 'Narrowing the Gap', worth £9.95, **plus** the Fabian Review environment special issue, **plus** the next two Fabian pamphlets. Call 020 7227 4900 or email us at info@fabian-society.org.uk for more information.

Fabian Review

www.fabians.org.uk

Winter 2008/09

NOW or NEVER

NOW MORE THAN EVER
...FAIRNESS IN A RECESSION

INTERVIEW
Roger Liddle
interviews Vince
Cable

JOHN McFALL
We must not stand
idly by

CITY BONUSES
New data on what
the public thinks
about the rich

The quarterly magazine of the Fabian Society Volume 120 no 4 £4.95

LABOUR PARTY
CONFERENCE ISSUE

Fabian Review

www.fabians.org.uk

Autumn 2008

MUST LABOUR LOSE?

THE **PROGRESSIVE FIGHTBACK**

PETER KELLNER: Labour's glimmers of hope | **DAVID LAMMY:** Britain is not broken
STELLA CREASY: Connect like Obama | **JON TRICKETT:** Messages for the marginals
JAMES PURNELL: Rediscover redistribution | **FIONA MACTAGGART:** Tax like we mean it
TIM HORTON: The Conservatives' confusion

The quarterly magazine of the Fabian Society   Volume 119 no 4   £4.95

Fabian Review

www.fabians.org.uk

Summer 2008

The Class Issue

THE GROWN UP GUIDE TO THE POLITICS OF CLASS

With David Blunkett, Danny Dorling, David Cannadine, Louise Bamfield and Sharon Hodgson.

The quarterly magazine of the Fabian Society   Volume 120 no 2   £4.95

The Fabian Review, Spring 2008

British Muslims and the politics of fairness

In 'Fairness not Favours', Sadiq Khan MP argues that an effective agenda to provide opportunity and tackle extremism across all communities must go beyond a narrow approach to security, and sets out new proposals for a progressive agenda on inequality and life chances, public engagement in foreign policy, an inclusive Britishness, and rethinking the role of faith in public life.

The pamphlet puts the case for an effective agenda to provide opportunity and tackle extremism across all communities must go beyond a narrow approach to security, and sets out new proposals for a progressive agenda on inequality and life chances, public engagement in foreign policy, an inclusive Britishness, and rethinking the role of faith in public life.

Special offer: join the Fabians for just £9.95 and get this book free.

'The Fabians ask the most difficult questions, pushing Labour to make a bold, progressive case on taxation and the abolition of child poverty.'
— Polly Toynbee

How can we make poverty history at home?

One in five children still grows up in poverty in Britain. Yet all the political parties now claim to care about 'social justice'. This report sets a litmus test by which Brown, Cameron and Campbell must be judged.

'Narrowing the Gap' is the final report of the Fabian Commission on Life Chances and Child Poverty, chaired by Lord Victor Adebowale. The Fabian Society is the only think tank with members. Join us and help us put poverty and equality at the centre of the political agenda.

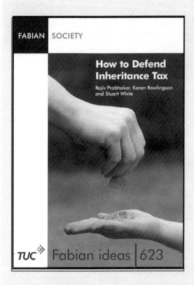

How to defend inheritance tax

Inheritance tax is under attack, and not just from the political right. The critics of this tax have dominated the debate over recent years but, as the authors of 'How to Defend Inheritance Tax' argue, this tax is one of the best tools we have for tackling inequality and kick starting Britain's stalled social mobility.

Defending inheritance tax is not just the responsibility of politicians – there must be a citizen-led campaign too. In this Fabian Ideas pamphlet, **Rajiv Prabhakar, Karen Rowlingson and Stuart White** provide progressives with the tools they need to win this argument.

They set out the evidence on inheritance and inequality, tackle the common objections to the tax, and demonstrate the moral and pragmatic arguments for an inheritance tax.

JOIN THE FABIANS TODAY
Join us and receive two Fabian Reviews, plus our award-winning equality report, 'Narrowing the Gap'

I'd like to become a Fabian for just £9.95

I understand that should at any time during my six-month introductory membership period I wish to cancel, I will receive a refund and keep all publications received without obligation. After six months I understand my membership will revert to the annual rate as published in *Fabian Review*, currently £31 (ordinary) or £14 (unwaged).

Name	Date of birth
Address	
	Postcode
Email	
Telephone	

Instruction to Bank   Originator's ID: 971666

Bank/building society name	
Address	**DIRECT Debit**
	Postcode
Acct holder(s)	
Acct no.	Sort code

I instruct you to pay direct debits from my account at the request of the Fabian Society. The instruction is subject to the safeguards of the Direct Debit Guarantee.

Signature	Date

Return to:
Fabian Society Membership
FREEPOST SW 1570
11 Dartmouth Street
London
SW1H 9BN